VOLUME TWO

Occult

THEOCRASY

The 1933 Classic

Lady Queenborough
EDITH STARR MILLER

DEFENDER

CRANE, MO

Occult Theocrasy: VOLUME II
By Lady Queenborough

Defender Publishing
Crane, MO 65633
©2018 this version by Thomas Horn

ISBN: 9781948014083

A CIP catalog record of this book is available from the Library of Congress.

Cover design by Jeffrey Mardis.

CONTENTS

Occult Theocrasy: Part II
Chronological Series
Associations of the 18th Century
(continued from Vol. 1)

Associations of the 19th Century

Associations of the 20th Century

ASSOCIATIONS OF THE 18TH CENTURY

continued from Vol. 1, Part II: Cronological Series

CHAPTER LV

THE UNITED IRISHMEN
(FOUNDED 1791)

IN 1791, THE Society of The United Irishmen was founded by Theobald Wolfe Tone and Napper Tandy, both of whom were high in rank in the Masonic lodges. The organization sought to unite Catholics, Protestants and Dissenters in order to throw off the oppressive yoke of England or, to use the graphic language of Tone himself, "to subvert the tyranny of our execrable government, to break the connection with England, the never-failing source of all our political evils, and to assert the independence of my country—these were my objects. To unite the whole people of Ireland."[1]

The priesthood and the nobles however stood solidly behind the English power; but the social conditions imposed by England on its Irish-Catholic subjects rendered that country a fertile soil for the sowing of the Revolutionary seed. These disabilities are described by Lecky in the following article which appeared in *Macmillan's Magazine*, January, 1873.

"To sum up briefly their provisions, they (the English) excluded the Catholics from the Parliament, from the magistracy, from the corporations, from the university, from the bench and from the bar, from the right of voting at parliamentary elections or at vestries of acting as constables, as sheriffs, or as jurymen, of serving in the army or navy, of becoming solicitors or even holding the position of gamekeeper or watchman. They prohibited them from becoming schoolmasters, ushers, or private tutors, or from sending their children abroad to receive the Catholic education they were refused at home. They offered an annuity to every priest who would forsake his creed, pronounced a sentence of exile against the whole hierarchy, and restricted the right of celebrating the mass to registered priests, whose number, according to the first intention of the Legislature, was not to be renewed. The Catholics could not buy land, or inherit or receive it as a gift from Protestants, or hold life annuities, or leases for more than thirty-one years, or any lease on such terms that the profits of the land exceeded one-third of the rent. A Catholic, except in the linen trade, could have no more than two apprentices. He could not have a horse of the value of more than £5, and any Protestant on giving him £5 might take his horse. He was compelled to pay double to the militia. In case of war with a Catholic Power, he was obliged to reimburse the damage done by the enemy's privateers. To convert a Protestant to Catholicism was a capital offence. No Catholic might marry a Protestant. Into his own family circle the elements of dissension were ingeniously introduced. A Catholic landowner might not bequeath his land as he pleased. It was divided equally among his children, unless the eldest son became a Protestant, in which case the parent became simply a life tenant, and lost all power either of selling or mortgaging it. If a Catholic's wife abandoned her husband's religion, she was immediately free from his control, and the Chancellor could assign her a certain proportion of her husband's property. If his child, however young, professed itself a Protestant, he was taken from his father's care, and the Chancellor could assign it a portion of its father's property. No Catholic could be guardian either to his own children or to those of another."

The investigations of R. C. Clifford detailed in his book *The Application of Jacobinism to the Secret Societies of Ireland and Great Britain* led this author to the conclusion that The United Irishmen and The Illuminati bore one another a close resemblance and, in his Diary, Wolfe Tone himself refers frankly to having on "several occasions pressed his friends the Jacobins to try to extend their clubs through the North."[2]

The history of the United Irishmen is largely the history of Theobald Wolfe Tone.

In a note to page 77 of his *Autobiography*, we are given the following information concerning the origin of The United Irishmen. "Before Tone's arrival in Belfast a political club, composed of Volunteers, and directed by a Secret Committee, was in existence. Among the members of the club were Neilson,[3] Russell, the Simses, Sinclair, McTier and Macabe after which Tone remarks "Mode of doing business by a Secret Committee, who are not known or suspected of co-operating, but who, in fact, direct the movements of Belfast."

After also drawing attention to the above, Captain Pollard in *The Secret Societies of Ireland*, page 14, proceeds to make the following observation:—"The enormous influence of the French revolution had begun to make itself felt in the councils of the secret associations, Jacobin missionaries spread the doctrine of the revolution, and a new spirit of militant republicanism was born. These emissaries from France aimed at bringing England low, and spreading the doctrine of world-revolution by means of an alliance between the Catholic malcontents of the south and the Republican Presbyterians of the north."

Suppressed in 1794, the order had reorganized in 1795 as a secret republican revolutionary society with subordinate societies and committees and had absorbed that of The Defenders.

John Keogh was the leader of the Roman Catholic branch of the movement among the other supporters of which were Archibald Hamilton Rowan, Robert Emmett, Thomas Addis Emmett, Arthur O'Connor and Lord Edward Fitzgerald.

In 1795, having become seriously implicated in the treasonable activities of the Rev. William Jackson, an emissary of the French Government to the Irish Revolutionaries, Tone went to America where he saw the French Minister Citizen Adet. With his approval and instructions, Wolfe Tone sailed for France on Jan. 1, 1796 where he spent the remainder of his days planning the downfall of England. He held that "unless they can separate England from Ireland, England is invulnerable."[4]

From the beginning of his French intrigues, he feared treason to his cause and, in his diary, we find the following entry dated March 21, 1796, quoting General Clark in a conversation he had just had with him:

"Even in the last war when the volunteers were in force" said the General "and a rupture between England and Ireland seemed likely, it was proposed in the French Council to offer assistance to Ireland, and overruled by the interest of Comte de Vergennes, then Prime Minister, who received for that service a considerable bribe from England, and that he (General Clark) was informed of this by a principal agent in paying the money. So, it seems, we had a narrow escape of obtaining our independence fifteen years ago. It is better as it is for then we were not united amongst ourselves, and I am not clear that the first use we should have made of our liberty would not have been to have begun cutting each other's throats: so out of evil comes good. I do not like this story of Vergennes, of the truth of which I do not doubt. How if the devil should put it into any one's head here to serve us so this time! Pitt is as cunning as hell, and he has money enough, and we have nothing but assignats; I do not like it at all…"[5]

Six months after his arrival in Paris, Tone received a commission in the French army, and with the assistance of the Directory, General Hoche and others organized the ill-fated Bantry Bay expedition of 1796. Every effort to thwart their plans was made by the French navy till, as Tone tells us in an entry dated Nov. 14 to 18, "Villaret de Joyeuse, the Admiral, is cashiered, and we have got another in his place. Joyeuse was giving, underhand, all possible impediment to our expedition."

His successor, Rear-Admiral Bruix, however, seems to have shared the indifference of his predecessor in Irish matters, and the fact that it was "always in their (the navy's) power to make us miscarry" is mentioned by Tone in his diary.

On Dec. 15, the expedition finally started and on the 17th, in a fog, the *Fraternité* with two of the Admirals and General Hoche aboard got separated from the rest of the fleet leaving Tone and General Grouchy with only about half of the original expeditionary force at their disposal.

Tone's efforts to effect a landing at Bantry Bay were frustrated by Grouchy's dilatory tactics and on Dec. 26 we find the following entry in Tone's Diary: "Last night, at half after six o'clock, in a heavy gale of wind still from the east, we were surprised by the Admiral's frigate running under our quarter, and hailing the *Indomptable* (Tone's ship) with orders to cut our cable and put to sea instantly; the frigate then pursued her course, leaving us all in the utmost astonishment."

Did Wolfe Tone think of Vergennes then? History fails to tell us!

The activities of The United Irishmen ended with the uprising of 1798 and another attempt by the French to land troops on Irish soil. This rebellion was however also crushed, and Wolfe Tone, who was taken prisoner and ordered to be hanged, cut his throat in his cell.

For root of this movement see Chapter LIII.

For development of this movement see Chapters LXIII, LXXXII, LXXXV, LXXXVIII.

CHAPTER LVI

THE ORANGE SOCIETY
(PROTESTANT AND MASONIC)
(FOUNDED 1795)

THE BATTLE OF the Diamond between the Peep-o'-Day Boys and the Defenders took place on Sept. 21, 1795.

We cannot improve on Captain Pollard's documented information in *The Secret Societies of Ireland* from which we quote:

"On the evening of the battle a number of the delegates of the Peep-o'-Day Boys met at the house of Thomas Wilson at Loughgall. There and then the name of the Society was changed to *The Orange Society*, and a grand lodge and subsidiary lodges initiated. The ritual was founded on Freemasonry (I° York Rite), and the legend was that of the Exodus of the Israelites.

"The original Peep-o'-Day Society had been confined to the lower orders, but with the change in Orangeism the upper classes began to take place and rank in the organization which was secretly fostered by the Government as a counter-poise against the seditious United Irishmen."[6]

"Prom 1828, the Orange Society was under the Grand Mastership of the Duke of Cumberland, and in 1835 there were no less than 140,000 Orangemen in England, 40,000 being in London alone. These members were not Irish Orangemen, but purely English, and they were engaged in a plot which recalls the best traditions of the Palais Royal and Philippe-Egalite. The purpose of the plot was to establish the Duke of Cumberland

7

as King of England, on the plea that William IV was still insane and the Princess Victoria a woman and a minor."[7]

"The revolutionary mechanism staged by the Orangemen was in many ways similar to that of the Orleanist party of Philippe. Wild rumours were set about. Colonel William Blennerhasset Fairman, Deputy Grand Secretary of the Orange Society, was the ruling spirit of the organization, and he conspired to such end that 381 loyal lodges were established in Great Britain. Another thirty were in the army, and branches were in many of the colonies.

"The conspiracy prospered from 1828 to 1835, when it was exposed by Mr. Hume, M. P., and a Committee of Enquiry in the Commons was granted. As the conspiracy, however, implicated half the Tory peers, some of the Bishops and most of the Army, everything passed off quietly; important witnesses vanished, and the Duke of Cumberland as Grand Master decreed the dissolution of the Orange Society in England without recourse to violence."

"The Volunteer movement began in 1914 in Ulster as the direct consequence of an attempt on the part of the Liberal Government to force the Home Rule Bill on that province. This unfortunate measure had passed the Houses despite the most rigid Unionist opposition, but Ulster had no intention of surrendering to its provisions without a struggle. The situation portended Civil War. A 'solemn League and Covenant', to resist it, was drawn up, and Ulster, organizing largely through the Orange Lodges, recruited an *Ulster Volunteer Force* which was completely organized throughout the North."

"The Orange Lodges had been reorganized in 1885, when Gladstone introduced the threatening Home Rule Bill. Prior to this the Order had somewhat relapsed and had been little more than a convivial friendly society. The threat of Home Rule brought it once more to the fore as a powerful political organization, and the Ulster electorate, which had until then been predominantly Liberal, became and remained solidly Unionist. The membership of the order expanded enormously, and the existing mechanism adapted itself to the new needs of the old motto, 'No surrender.'

"The Orange Lodges had been legally drilling since January 5, 1912, when application was made to the Belfast Justices for leave to drill on behalf of Colonel R. H. Wallace, C. B., Grand Master of the Belfast and Grand Secretary of the Provincial Grand Lodge of Ulster; but, the skeleton organization had long been in existence, as was evident by the splendidly disciplined marching of the Lodges at the great Craigavon meeting in Sept. 1911.[8]

The Ulster Volunteers, under Sir Edward Carson, rejected all suggestions for partition and proclaimed their intention of smashing once and for all the whole Home Rule movement.

The Irish Volunteers while claiming Home Rule refused to consent to the exclusion of Ulster on the ground that Ulster being Ireland it should remain Ireland, thus annulling all the efforts of Mr. Asquith, England's Prime Minister, to effect a compromise.

Further quoting Pollard: "Affairs became more and more chaotic and at last John Redmond, the leader of the Home Rule party, realized in some measure what a menace the Irish Volunteer movement was becoming." He decided to attempt to control them... He tried to raise funds for the advertised purpose of purchasing arms at some future date, but before this came about the members of the original committee purchased a stock of serviceable weapons with money supplied by the Irish Republican Brotherhood and succeeded in running the cargoes in at Kilcool and Howth."[9]

Then came the declaration of war between Britain and Germany and the part played by Ireland during the World war is a matter of history.

Interlocked with the history of the Irish Republican Brotherhood, The Clan-na-Gael and Sinn Fein, the activities of this society after 1914 can be followed in the articles on these other organizations.

For root of this movement see Chapter LV.

For development of this movement see Chapter's LXXXVII I and CXVI.

CHAPTER LVII

THE PHILADELPHIANS
(THE OLYMPIANS)
(FOUNDED 1798)

THE PHILADELPHIANS, A Royalist Anti-Bonapartist Secret Society, was founded on masonic lines about 1798 at Besançon, France, by General Malet and organized by a Freemason, Lieutenant Colonel Oudet.

Using England as a base of operations, it cooperated for a while with the "Chouans" whose chief, Pichegru, was eventually captured and executed by order of the Directory.

After this event, the Philadelphians adopted the name of The Olympians. Most of them however, including Oudet, were shot from ambush the day after the battle of Wagram, the responsibility for their deaths being placed on Napoleon I.

In 1812 General Malet formed a conspiracy to overthrow the Empire. Among those implicated were Generals Moreau, Talleyrand, Trochot, the Comte de Noailles, the Comte de Montmorency and Fouche, who was then under the cloud of Napoleon's displeasure. General Masséna, Grand Master of the Grand Orient, who at that time was in disgrace, was to have been offered the command of the troops. This daring plot almost succeeded and Fouche says that Malet carried with him to the grave "the

11

secret of one of the boldest conspiracies which the Grand Epoch of the Revolution has bequeathed to history."[10]

General Moreau, who had gone to settle in America returned to France in 1813, the last of the leaders of the Olympians. He died Sept. 2 from a wound received some days earlier.

A few moments after the death of Moreau, the Senate pronounced the deposition of Napoleon and carried out the programme of the Olympians.

CHAPTER LVIII

THE SCOTTISH PHILOSOPHIC RITE
(FOUNDED 1799)

REV. E. CAHILL, S. J., in his book *Freemasonry and the Anti-Christian Movement*, page 143, names The Scottish Philosophic Rite as one of the principal divisions of Freemasonry, and he writes:

"*The Scottish Philosophic Rite* is practised by the Masons subject to the Lodge Alpina in Switzerland. This latter Grand Lodge, which is among those formally recognized by the Grand Lodges of the British Isles, is of special importance, as it is not unfrequently utilised as a kind of liaison body by the different rites and lodges of the several jurisdictions all over the world in their negotiations with each other."

For root of this movement see Chapter XLVI.

ASSOCIATIONS OF THE 19TH CENTURY

CHAPTER LIX

MODERN KNIGHTS TEMPLAR ENGLAND
(FOUNDED 1804)

IN AN ADDRESS by Col. W. J. B. Macleod Moore, of the Grand Cross of the Temple Royal Arch, Grand Prior of the Dominion of Canada, printed in *The Rosicrucian and Masonic Record* (page 165), we obtain the following salient points of English Templar history:

"In 1791, we find the Templar Rite styled 'Grand Elect Knights Templar Kadosh, of St. John of Jerusalem, Palestine, Rhodes, and Malta', thus combining the modern and more ancient titles... In 1848 after the Ancient and Accepted Scottish Rite of 33° had been established in England, the Templar body resigned control over the Rose Croix and Kadosh, which had been incorporated into the Ancient and Accepted Rite as the 18th and 30th degrees. It was therefore necessary to suppress the old ceremonies and confine themselves to the Templar alone and to change the name into the degree of 'Masonic Knights Templar'. This title was not used in England before 1851, although the term Masonic appears in the warrants of Admiral Dunkerley between 1791[11] and 1796... Until 1853 the Order of the Temple and Malta remained combined.

"In 1863 the Grand Conclave again formally revived the Maltese Order, with a considerable ritual, but as a separate degree instead of combined with the Templars as it had been before 1853."

The following, borrowed from *The History of Freemasonry and Concordant Orders*, a work by Stillson and Hughan, reputed authorities on Masonic matters, gives us the history of Modern English Templarism.

"In 1867–68 a proposal was promulgated to unite the branches of the Order in England, Ireland and Scotland, under one head; and H. R. H. the Prince of Wales, who had been initiated into Masonry and the Templar degree in Sweden, consented, in 1869, to assume the Grand Mastership of the Templars of the United Kingdom. On the 7th April, 1873, H. R. H. was installed Grand Master… This assumption by H. R. H. the Prince of Wales, to use the words of the Arch-Chancellor of the Order, Sir Patrick Colquhoun, 'effected a perfect reformation of the Order, and procured for it a status it had hitherto not enjoyed, even under the Duke of Kent, who must be practically regarded as its founder, with the additional advantage of H. R. H. being at once head of the Craft and Temple; indeed, it may be said that as the Order was reformed in 1804–7 by the Duke of Kent, so it was again re-founded under his grandson, the Prince of Wales, in 1873'. At this date the Order assumed the name of United Religious and Military Order of the Temple and of St. John of Jerusalem, Palestine, Rhodes and Malta." Macleod Moore informs us that in 1813 the Craft degrees, including the 'Royal Arch', were alone recognized as pure and ancient Freemasonry and that the possession of the Royal Arch degree in modern times has been, and is now, considered quite sufficient to preserve the link between the Temple Order and Freemasonry.

CHAPTER LX

MODERN KNIGHTS TEMPLAR FRANCE
(FOUNDED 1804)

HECKETHORN IN HIS well-known book *Secret Societies of all Ages and Countries* gives the following graphic description of the foundation of this order.

"We read that several lords of the Court of Louis XIV, including the Duke de Gramont, the Marquis of Biran, and Count Tallard, formed a secret society, whose object was pleasure. The society increased. Louis XIV, having been made acquainted with its statutes, banished the members of the Order, whose denomination was, 'A slight Resurrection of the Templars.'

"In 1705, Philippe, Duke of Orleans,[12] collected the remaining members of the society that had renounced its first scope to cultivate politics. A Jesuit father, Bonanni, a learned rogue, fabricated the famous list of supposititious Grand Masters of the Temple since Molay, beginning with his immediate successor, Larmenius. No imposture was ever sustained with greater sagacity. The document offered all the requisite characteristics of authenticity, and was calculated to deceive the most experienced palæologist. Its object was to connect the new institution with the ancient Templars. To render the deception more perfect, the volume containing the false list was filled with minutes of deliberations at fictitious meetings under false dates. Two members were even sent to Lisbon, to obtain if possible a document of legitimacy from the 'Knights of Christ', an Order supposed to have been founded on the ruins of the Order of the Temple. But the deputies were unmasked and very badly received: one had to take refuge in England, the other was transported to Africa, where he died.

"But the society was not discouraged; it grew, and was probably the same that concealed itself before the outbreak of the revolution under the vulgar name of the Society of the Bull's Head and whose members were dispersed in 1792. At that period the Duke of Cossé-Brissac was Grand Master. When on his way to Versailles with other prisoners, there to undergo their trial, he was massacred, and Ledru, his physician, obtained possession of the charter of Larmenius and the MS. statutes of 1705. These documents suggested to him the idea of reviving the order; Fabre-Palaprat, a Freemason, was chosen grand master. Every effort was made to create a belief in the genuineness of the Order. The brothers Fabré, Arnal, and Leblond hunted up relics. The shops of antiquaries supplied the sword, mitre, and helmet of Molay, and the faithful were shown his bones, withdrawn from the funeral pyre on which he has been burned."[13]

This presumably is the particular Templar sect that furnished Isaac Long with all the Templar bric-a-brac that found its way to Charleston in 1804.

"As in the Middle Ages, the society exacted that aspirants should be of noble birth; such as were not were ennobled by it. Fourteen honest citizens of Troyes on one occasion received patents of nobility and convincing coats of arms."

The order founded its first Lodge on Dec. 23, 1805, deriving from the Grand Orient of France.

From 1805 to 1815, the brother Francisco Alvaro da Silva, Knight of the Order of Christ, secret agent in Paris of John VI of Portugal, was a member of the order. He knew its secret history from its organizers, and in 1812 became its Chief Secretary.

In 1814, Fabré-Palaprat found a Greek manuscript of the 15th century, containing a chapter of St. John the Evangelist which conflicted on many points with the Gospel inserted in the canons of the Roman Church and preceded by a sort of introduction and commentary entitled

Leviticon. He forthwith determined to appropriate this doctrine to his order, which was thus transformed from a perfectly orthodox association into a schismatic sect. The author of this work was a monk at Athens called Nicephorus. He was a member of the Sufi sect, one which professes the doctrines of the Ancient Lodge of Cairo.

"Those knights that adopted its doctrines made them the basis of a new liturgy, which they rendered public in 1833 in a kind of Johannite church."

The Order of the Temple of Paris described by Heckethorn, as stated above, gives a list of the names of the successors of Jacques de Molay as follows. Other Templars, who do not admit the legality of the Grand Mastership of Larmenius, give different lists of Grand Masters:

- John Mark Larmenius   1314
- Thomas Theobald Alexandrinus   1324
- Arnold de Braque   1340
- John de Claremont   1349
- Bertrand du Guesclin   1357
- John Arminiaeus   1381
- Bertrand Arminiaeus   1392
- John Arminiaeus   1419
- John de Croy   1451
- Bernard Imbault   1472
- Robert Senoncourt   1478
- Galeatino de Salazar   1497
- Philip Chabot   1516
- Gaspard de Jaltiaco Tavanensis   1544
- Henry de Montmorency   1574
- Charles de Valois   1615
- James Ruxellius de Granceio   1651
- Duc de Duras   1681
- Philippe Duc d'Orléans   1705
- Duc de Maine   1724
- Louis Henry Bourbon   1737

- Louis Francis Bourbon   1741
- Duc de Cosse Brissac   1776
- Claude M. R. Chevillon   1792
- Bernard R. Fabré-Palaprat   1804
- Admiral Sir Sidney Smith   1838 to 1840

This list is quoted from a manuscript of A. G. Mackey in the possession of the writer.

CHAPTER LXI

MODERN KNIGHTS TEMPLAR SWEDEN

STILLSON AND HUGHAN, giving no date of foundation, state that:

"The Swedish Templars assert that Templary was introduced there by a nephew of De Molay, who was a member of the new Order of Christ in Portugal, and they now, with Denmark and other nationalities of Germany, practised the reformed system of the obsolete Templar rite of the 'Strict Observance'."[14]

'Strict Observance' was Templarism.

For root of this movement see Chapter XLIV.

CHAPTER LXII

RITE OF MIZRAIM
(FOUNDED 1805)

THIS RITE HAD 90 degrees. It was founded in 1805 at Milan by Le Changeur, Clavel, Marc Bedarride and Joly, and was introduced into France in 1816.

Its trials of initiation were long and difficult, and founded on what is recorded of the Egyptian and Eleusinian mysteries.

Heckethorn states that this rite is essentially autocratic there being no obligation on the Grand Master to account for his actions.

In the *Rosicrucian* for January 1871 we read the following notice (page 136).

"We have great pleasure in announcing that this philosophic Masonic Rite (Ancient and Primitive Rite of Mizraim) has been recently established in England under authority derived from the Grand Council of Rites for France, and that the Conservators General held a meeting at Freemasons Tavern, on Wednesday, the 28th December. The principal chairs were filled by Ill. Bros. Wentworth Little 90°; the Rt. Hon. The Earl of Limerick 90°; and S. Rosenthal 90°; by whom the 'Bective' Sanctuary of Levites—the 33rd of the Rite—was duly opened...

It was then announced that the following brethren had accepted office in the Rite: The Rt. Hon. the Earl of Bective, Sovereign Grand Master, etc., etc."

The Rite of Mizraim was amalgamated with that of Memphis in 1775, when John Yarker, as stated by Freke Gould[15] "sanctioned the communication of the degrees of Mizraim to members of the Rite of Memphis, the former having no separate governing body in this country" (England).

"According to an official statement, repeated in every number of the Kneph:" France (having) abandoned the Rite, and the Ill. Gd. Hierophant, J. E. Marconis, 33°, 97°, having died in 1868, Egypt took full possession. The Craft Gd. Lodge, our Antient and Primitive Rite, and the Antient and Accepted Rite, executed a tripartite Treaty to render mutual aid, and restored the Sov. Gd. Mystic Temple—Imp. Council Cen., 96°, presided over by a Gd. Hierophant, 97°, in 1775."

Essentially Jewish, the historical activities of this order to date are interesting.

Some years ago, a document to which the reader must be referred, *The Protocols of the Wise Men or Elders of Zion*,[16] was brought to light. Abstracted from a Jewish Lodge of Mizraim in Paris, in 1884, by Joseph Schorst, later murdered in Egypt, it embodied the programme of esoteric Judaism. Schorst was the son of a man who, in 1881, had been sentenced in London to ten years penal servitude for counterfeiting.

Before studying these *Protocols* however, the reader should be made acquainted with a few facts.

This document was first published in 1905 at Tsarskoe Selo (Russia), embodied in a book called *The Great Within the Small* written by Sergius A. Nilus.

In January 1917, a second edition, revised and documented, was ready, but before it could be put on the market for distribution and sale, the revolution had taken place (March 1917), and the Provisional Government had been replaced by that of Kerensky who himself gave the order to have the whole edition of S. A. Nilus's book destroyed. It was burnt.

A few copies however had been distributed, one of them found its way to England, one to Germany and one again to the United States of America in 1919. In each of these three countries, a few people determined to make a close study of the document with the result that it was soon published everywhere.

In England, it was and still is published by an organization called "The Britons".

In Germany, a remarkable work was done by Gottfried zum Beck.

In France, it was published by Mgr. Jouin of the *Revue Internationale des Societes Secretes* and by the fearless M. Urbain Gohier of *Vieille France*.

In the United States, two anonymous editions were published, one by Small Maynard of Boston, and the other, later, by the Beckwith Company.

Then editions appeared in Italian, Russian, Arabic and even Japanese.

No sooner had the document been made public than loud protests were heard coming from all sections of dispersed Israel. Writers and lecturers were recruited to deny the assertion and shatter the growing belief of a Jewish conspiracy for the political, economic and legislative dominion of the world.

The method of intimidation used to suppress discussion of *The Protocols* has always been the same. It consists in suggesting that the person guilty of interest in the subject is crazy or becoming so. As the average mortal prefers to be thought sane by his fellow men, the trick generally works.

A short review of the affray must be made. First and foremost came a strong denial made by a Jew, Lucien Wolf, who wrote the pamphlet: *The Jewish Bogey and the Forged Protocols of the Learned Elders of Zion*, (1920). Israel Zangwill, another Jew, also wrote against the veracity of the *Protocols*. Then, in America, followed articles by William Hard, in the *Metropolitan*, ridiculing belief in the document.

More serious was the painstaking campaign undertaken against the publication of the *Protocols* by the chiefs of the U. S. Kahal or Kehillah, who intimidated the editor, George H. Putnam, and. forced him to stop the publication of the book by threats to call his loans and thus ruin him financially. The Beckwith Co. was eventually induced by the Jewish Anti-Defamation League to enclose in every copy of the edition they published a small pamphlet containing the denial of the contents of the *Protocols*.

Among the Gentiles found ready to deny the truth of the *Protocols* was a certain du Chayla, also a Mrs. Hurlbut and the notorious Princess

Catherine Radziwill who had previously reached the pinnacle of self-advertisement by having had herself sentenced to a term of imprisonment in South Africa for forgery in 1902. It seemed as if all the denials against the Jewish authorship of the *Protocols* had been made, when finally in 1921 the London Times made the sensational discovery through one of its correspondents in Constantinople, a Mr. X.—of a French book which they called the *Dialogues of Geneva*, published anonymously at Brussels in 1865. It was this book, the Times affirmed, which had been plagiarized by the author of the *Protocols*.

The publication of this discovery by the Times seemed to have closed all further discussion tending to prove the Jewish authenticity of the *Protocols* and very little has been heard since on the subject.

Yet, to use the words of the Zionist, Max Nordau, during his violent quarrel with another Zionist, Asher Ginzberg: *Audealur et altera pars*. It is this other side of the story which the reader is now asked to hear.

The book *The Times* called *The Geneva Dialogues* bears in reality the following title: *Dialogues aux Enfers entre Machiavelli et Montesquieu*. It had been published anonymously in Brussels in 1864. The introduction ends thus: "Geneva, October 13, 1865".

It was soon discovered by the police of Napoleon III that the author of the book was a certain lawyer, Maurice Joly, who was arrested, tried, and sentenced to two years' imprisonment (April 1865), as it was averred that he had written his book as an attack against the government of Napoleon III to which he had lent all the Machiavelian plans revealed in the *Dialogues*.

A short sketch of the author's life is necessary in order to understand the spirit of his book.

Maurice Joly (1831–1878), was born at Lons-le-Saulnier. His mother, nee Florentine Corbara Courtois, was a Corsican of Italian origin and a Roman Catholic. Her father, Laurent Courtois, had been paymaster-general of Corsica. He had an inveterate hatred of Napoleon I.

Joly's father was Philipe Lambert Joly, born at Dieppe, Normandy. He had a comfortable fortune and had been attorney general for the department of Jura for a period of 10 years under Louis Philippe. Maurice Joly was educated at Dijon and began his law studies there, but in 1849 he left for Paris.

There, thanks to his maternal grandfather's masonic associations, he secured, just before the Coup d'Etat in 1851, a post in the Ministry of the Interior under M. Chevreau. In 1860 only, he terminated his law studies,—he wrote several articles, showed a certain amount of talent and ended by founding a paper called *Le Palais* for lawyers and attorneys. The principal stockholders were Jules Favre, Desmaret, Leblond, Adolphe Cremieux, Arago, and Berryer.

Joly was a Socialist. He wrote of himself: "Socialism seems to me one of the forms of a new life for the peoples emancipated from the traditions of the Old World. I accept a great many of the solutions offered by Socialism but I reject Communism either as a social factor or as a political institution. Communism is but a school of Socialism. In politics I understand extreme means to gain one's ends—in that, at least, I am a Jacobin." Friend of Adolphe Cremieux, he shared in his hatred of Napoleon III. He hated absolutism as much as he hated Communism and as, under the influence of his Prime Minister Rouher, the French Emperor led a policy of reaction, Maurice Joly qualified it as Machiavelian and depicted it as such in his pamphlet.

In one of his books he wrote of it:

"Machiavelli represents the policy of Might compared to Montesquieu's, which represents the policy of Right—Machiavelli will be Napoleon III who will himself depict his abominable policy". (From Maurice Joly—*Son passe, son programme*—by himself, 1870).

And here comes the important point which the *Times* omitted to put before its readers when it made the sensational discovery about the Dialogues of Geneva in 1921!

Maurice Joly, who hated Communism and, in 1864, ascribed the Machiavelian policy of Might over Right to the Imperialism of Napoleon III, was evidently ignorant of the fact that he himself was no innovator, for, long before he ever entered the journalistic or political world, the very theory which he had tried to expose and refute had been the guiding principle of a group of ardent revolutionists, promoters of Communism, and worthy followers of Illuminatis and Babouvists, the group of Karl Marx, Jacoby, etc. the agitators of the 1848 revolution.

Long before Maurice Joly's book *Dialogues aux Enfers entre Machiavelli et Montesquieu* had made its appearance, another book bearing much the same title had been published in Berlin in 1850. It was called *Machiavelli, Montesquieu, Rousseau* by Jacob Venedy and was published by Franz Dunnicker, Berlin.[17]

Jacob Venedy, the author, was a Jew, born in Cologne, May 1805, died February 1871. Owing to his revolutionary activities, he was expelled from Germany and sought refuge in France. "While living in Paris, in 1835, he edited a paper of subversive character called *he Proscrit* which caused the police to send him away from Paris. He then lived at Le Hâvre. Later, due to the intercession of Arago and Mignet, friends of Adolphe Cremieux, he was once more allowed to return to Paris. Meanwhile, he had published a book, *Romanisme, Christianisme et Germanisme*, which had won for him the praise of the French Academy. Venedy was a close friend and associate of Karl Marx. He had spent the years 1843–44 in England which at that time was the refuge and abode of all the master minds of the 1848 revolution. In 1847 Venedy was in Brussels with Karl Marx who had founded there the secret organization called "The Communist League of Workers", which was eventually brought out into the open under the name of "The International Society of Democracy" (*Societe Internationale de la Democratic*).

In 1848, after the February Revolution, Venedy returned to Germany, still in the company of Karl Marx. He soon afterwards became one of the chiefs of the revolutionary Committee of Fifty, organized at Frankfort-on-Main in March 1848. Venedy was sent as "Commissar" into the Oberland to stand against Ecker. In Hesse-Homburg he was elected a member of the Left and took his place in the Committee of Fifty. It was at this time that in Berlin he published his book *Machiavelli, Montesquieu and Rousseau*, upholding the ideas of Machiavelli and Rousseau for the slavery and demoralization of the people.

When order was once more re-established in Germany, Venedy was expelled from Berlin and Breslau.

He was an active member of the Masonic Order Bauhlitte which was affiliated to the Carbonari. (See *Die Bauhlütte* for Feb. 25, 1871).

It is to be regretted that the *Times*, which had started an investigation to trace the authorship of *The Protocols of the Wise Men of Zion*, and lift it off the shoulders of Jewry upon which it rested, should have missed looking into the literary and revolutionary activities of Jacob Venedy.

Following the apparent contradiction between Jacob Venedy and Maurice Joly, one showing the Machiavelli and Rousseau policy as that of triumphant Communism, whilst the other makes it the policy of Reaction and Imperialism, one is apt to overlook the link between the two. The student of the 1830–1848 period of history is here confronted by a remarkable fact.

Fould, the Rothschilds of Paris, London and Vienna, Montefiore, Disraeli, the Goldsmids, were not less Jews than Karl Marx, Moses Hess, Jacoby, Lassalle, Venedy, and Riesser. The Liberal Conservatism of Disraeli, the reactionary Imperialism of Fould and the revolutionary Communism of Karl Marx all point towards the same aim, namely, the establishment of Jewish power, whether under a Constitutional Monarchy, an Empire, or a Republic. And although their respective activities seem to stand so far apart, yet they are all linked, all tending towards the same end. One of the most striking instances is the case of Adolphe Cremieux who played a prominent part in the period we are now concerned with, and who was connected with all parties and actually helped form the centre which united them all, viz. The *Alliance Israelite Universelle*, which was, in fact, the central Kahal for Universal Jewry.

The life of Adolphe Cremieux and the activities of his Jewish contemporaries, belonging to widely divergent social spheres, illustrate forcibly the concerted plan of Judaism to reach its secret Messianic hope of world domination.

Until about 1848, it seemed somewhat difficult to show conclusively the link between Judaism and Illuminism, Communism and Capitalism, but a close study of the life of Adolphe Cremieux, and that of his confidential agent, Leon Gambetta, throws full light on the subject.

Whereas in Gentile life, there is an unbridgeable abyss between

Conservatism and Anarchy, Religion and Atheism, there is no such chasm in the Jewish mentality. There, all currents, no matter in what direction they may seem to flow, are finally united and channeled in one unique direction.

If it has been somewhat difficult for historians of the French Revolution to see the close link between Judaism and Illuminism, we repeat that no such difficulty exists for the student of the 1848 revolutionary period, after he has followed the life of Adolphe Crémieux and the activities of his Jewish contemporaries. The main difference is that the term "Illuminism" used in the 18th century is replaced by the wide term Freemasonry which embraces all the existent secret societies.

Adolphe Isaac Cremieux (1796–1880) came from a Jewish family of the South of France that had members in Aix, Nîmes and Marseilles.[18]

In his youth, Cremieux was an enthusiastic admirer of Napoleon I; yet in 1831, he pronounces the funeral eulogy of the ill-famed revolutionist of 1789, the Abbe Gregoire. He chose law as his profession and was admitted to the Bar at Nimes in 1817.

Briefly, Cremieux's life may be viewed from three sides: 1st, his racial Jewish activities, 2nd, his Masonic activities, 3rd, his political influence.

Cremieux's racial Jewish activities are exemplified by the part he took in the Damascus Affair with Moses Montefiore, a Jew of England, when Jewry successfully but unconvincingly silenced the accusation of ritual murder committed upon the Catholic priest, Father Thomas, at Damascus, in 1840. He had a prominent share in the foundation and development of the *Alliance Israelite Universelle*. Officially founded in 1860, this international union of disseminated Jewry had, as we know, existed for centuries, but after the Damascus affair, the Jewish leaders knew that they had attained sufficient power to feel enabled to show to the whole world that although the civil rights they enjoyed had been granted them by different countries, the real allegiance of each and every one of them was due to their Jewish nationality.

The Masonic activities of Adolphe Cremieux were many and powerful. His connection with Louis Bonaparte and his brother, who both were affiliated to the Carbonari, would suggest that he was also connected with this secret society. But it is a fact that Cremieux belonged to the Lodge of Mizraim, the Scottish Rite, and also the Grand Orient. He was in the Supreme Council of the Order of Mizraim and, at the death of Viennet, in whose person the Grand Orient and the Scottish Rite had been united, Cremieux succeeded him as Grand Master.

The political activities of Cremieux are also manifold and varied. In his youth, he had been an admirer of Napoleon I and later became an intimate friend as well as the legal adviser of the Bonaparte family and joined their party which was undermining the government of Louis Philippe, son of Philippe "Egalite".

In 1848, he was one of the most ardent supporters of Louis Napoleon and took an active part in the overthrow of Louis Philippe. He had been one of the foremost speakers in the association known as the *Campagne des Banquets* which had done so much to promote the Revolution of Feb. 1848.

He became a member of the provisional government and was appointed Minister of Justice. He strongly advocated the candidature of his friend, Louis Napoleon, for the post of President of the French Republic. Cremieux had had hopes of being made Chief Executive under Louis Napoleon and thus play in France the same role which Disraeli played in England that is ruling the country from behind the scenes. Both Disraeli and Cremieux had the same financial backing, namely the wealth of the Rothschilds and Montefiores who, in London, were friends of Disraeli and, in Paris, friends of Cremieux. Cremieux was therefore keenly disappointed when General Cavaignac was appointed Prime Minister in the Republican Government of Louis Napoleon, and as a revenge, he directed his activities against the Prince President, his former friend. He became so hostile to him that in 1851, after the Coup d'Etat of December 2, by which Louis Napoleon recreated the Empire and assumed the title of Napoleon III, Cremieux was imprisoned at Vincennes and Mazas. After his release, he made himself the champion and defender of the Communist associates of Karl Marx, the revolutionaries Louis Blanc, Ledru Rollin, Pierre Leroux and others.

His untiring efforts were directed against the Empire in general and

Napoleon III in particular, and he consorted with all the Emperor's enemies, among them, Maurice Joly, the author of the *Dialogue between Machiavelli and Montesquieu*. After the overthrow of Napoleon III and the defeat of France at the hands of Germany in 1871, and the establishment of the Republic, Cremieux once more took an open part in the political affairs of the country.

He pushed to the front his former secretary Gambetta and effectively directed him in his shady negotiations with Bismarck, the latter himself being guided by the Jew Bamberger (1852–1899), a former revolutionist of 1848, but who, having found refuge in France, had been for many years manager in Paris of the Jewish Bank Bischoffsheim and Goldschmidt. He was one of Cremieux's friends, and the war could not affect the ties linking the Jews united in the *Alliance Israelite Universelle*.

From 1871 until his death, it can be safely asserted that Cremieux as President of the *Alliance Israelite Universelle* and Grand Master of the *Scottish Rile*, exercised a tremendous influence upon the anti-religious campaign which followed the Franco-Prussian War. In this as in all his lifelong activities, Cremieux was only obeying the teachings of the Talmud and trying to destroy every religion but that contained in Judaism. His favourite theme was that there should be only one cult—and that cult should be Jewish. At a general assembly of the *Alliance Israelite Universelle*, on May 31 1864, Cremieux had said: "The Alliance is not limited to our cult, it voices its appeal to all cults and wants to penetrate in all the religions as it has penetrated into all countries. Let us endeavour boldly to bring about the union of all cults under one flag of Union and Progress. Such is the slogan of humanity."[19]

One cult, one flag! Are the *Protocols of the Wise Men of Zion* or the speeches of Machiavelli in Joly's book anything but a lengthy exposition of the ideas briefly expressed by Cremieux? His activities are one of the clearest examples of Jewish internationalism and Jewish efforts for the realization of the Messianic ideal.

The *Alliance Israelite Universelle* issued from the Rite of Mizraim plus Universal Freemasonry, subsidized by International Finance, would spell the doom of Christian civilization, the destruction of nationalism, the death of nations upon whose ruin has been erected a new Temple of Solomon, containing the treasures and material wealth of the whole world, and over which is placed the six pointed star of ZIONISM.[20]

Leon Gambetta (1838–1882) an Italian Jew, obtained French naturalization on Oct. 29, 1859, and in 1862 became the secretary of Cremieux. He was *Depute* in 1869, Dictator of National Defence, head of the War Office and Minister of the Interior after the Commune of 1870 and Dictator again after the Coup d'Etat of the President of the Republic Marshal MacMahon in 1877. The following quotation from a letter which he wrote to his father on June 22, 1863 is interesting.

"My chief, Maitre Cremieux, treats me as if I were his adopted son, and if within three years' time he is elected a deputy (which is quite possible) my career will be settled once and for all. I must devote myself to law and politics, and then I may hope to triumph over all obstacles and finally to attain great honours."[21]

CHAPTER LXIII

THE RIBBON SOCIETY
(Roman Catholic)
(Founded 1805)

THIS SOCIETY APPEARED about 1805–1807.

We are again indebted to Captain Pollard for a sketch of its history: "After the suppression of the United Irishmen the society, as such, disappeared, but within a year or two we find a renaissance of the old agrarian Catholic secret societies which had been absorbed into the Defenders and thence into the United Irishmen. The provisions of the Insurrection Act which forbade the possession of arms and enforced a curfew at nightfall were in operation until 1805, when with its relaxation appears the *Ribbon Society...* In different counties local organizations of Ribbon men called themselves by different titles, such as the Threshers, the Carders, the Molly Maguires, Rockites, Caravats, Shanavests, Pauddeen Gar's men and the like."[22]

The Ribbon Society "continued the system of organization used by the United Irishmen. A lodge was limited to forty members and they met as a rule in the fields by night, armed sentinels being posted to guard the spot. The lodge was under a Master or Body Master, who controlled three committee-men, each of whom was responsible for twelve members of the lodge. The Masters were represented on divisional committees allocated on the basis of four or more divisions to a geographical county.

The divisional committees were controlled by Parish Masters, who in turn were represented on the County Council, which contributed two delegates to the National Board.[23]

"As Whiteboys they certainly were at political and practical war with the Orangemen, and throughout their activities appear to have been criminal and antisocial; outrage, terrorism and murder being their only methods of political conversion."[24]

For root of this movement see Chapter LV.

CHAPTER LXIV

THE CERNEAU RITE
(ANCIENT AND ACCEPTED SCOTTISH RITE)
(FOUNDED 1808)

THE FOLLOWING ARTICLE is quoted in part from an article specifically written by Josiah H. Drummond 33° in *The History of Freemasonry and Concordant Orders* by Stillson and Hughan:[25]

"In 1806 Joseph Cerneau appeared in New York; he had been a member of Masonic bodies in the West Indies; he had a patent from Mathieu Dupotet certifying that he had received the degrees of the Scottish Rite of Heredom, and authorizing him to confer the degrees up to the Twenty-fourth and organize bodies in the northern part of Cuba, and to confer the Twenty-fifth on one person in each year, the Twenty-fifth being then the highest degree of the Rite and the highest Cerneau had received, according to his patent. Cerneau had his patent from Dupotet, who had his from Germain Hacquet, who had his from Du Plessis, who had his from Prevost in 1790, who had his from Francken."[26]

In 1808 he called a grand consistory of the Rite of Heredom having jurisdiction over 25 degrees.

"But already a controversy had arisen with parties acting under, or deriving their powers from, the Supreme Council at Charleston. We may well believe that Cerneau and his associates soon recognized the impossibility of maintaining successfully a rite of *twenty-five* degrees against one of *thirty-three* degrees... The Thirty-third degree as now existing originated at Charleston in 1801; and no evidence has been found that Cerneau ever received it."

Cerneau seems however to have overlooked the obvious expedient of creating a 34th degree!

"The Charleston body did not recognize the Cerneau Bodies even by silent acquiescence; after investigation by a special Deputy, it declared, early in 1814, Cerneau to be an impostor, and his organizations illegal and clearly clandestine."

"Bitter controversies followed." Lodges which soon died were opened at Charleston. Others at New Orleans eked out a precarious existence under James Foulhouze. "Foulhouze had received the Thirty-third degree from the Grand Orient of France, which expelled him, Feb. 4, 1859, for a scurrilous publication which he issued in answer to one of its decrees. This Supreme Council became dormant; but, in 1867, it was revived with Eugene Chassaignac at its head; in 1868 it was recognized by the Grand Orient of France, and unless it has recently gone out of existence, the Grand-Orient today recognizes a so-called Supreme Council in New Orleans as a lawful body, and its members as possessing the Thirty-third degree!"

In 1826 the Morgan murder occurred and Cerneau left for France. De Witt Clinton, Governor of New York, had been Deputy Grand Commander of the Sovereign Consistory from 1811 to 1823 when he was elected Grand Commander.

A number of sporadic revivals of this rite occurred during the ensuing 40 years.

They were known as—

- The Hicks Rite, founded in 1832 by Comte de St. Laurent.
- The First Atwood Body, founded about 1837 by Henry C. Atwood.
- The Cross Body, founded about 1851 by Jeremy L. Cross.
- The Second Atwood Body, founded about 1853.

It was not till 1867 that peace was established between the three *de facto* Supreme Councils in the northern part of the United States. On that date they united and Josiah H. Drummond was elected Grand Commander.

After five years of peace, however, Henry J. Seymour, who had been expelled by the council of which he was a member, organized what he called a Supreme Council of which he was made Grand Commander, "but, on a visit to Europe in 1862, in his eagerness to obtain recognition, he unwittingly held Masonic communication with the Grand Orient of France, which created such a storm that he resigned his office, and since but little has been heard of that Supreme Council, although it probably still exists."

"In 1881, Hopkins Thompson, an *Emeritus* member of the Supreme Council, assisted by a few Honorary members and by a Sublime Prince of the Royal Secret, who is believed by many to have been the mainspring of the movement, all of whom had taken the oath of fealty to the Supreme Council, formed an association, which they are pleased to call the Cerneau Supreme Council 'revived'."

"This body claims jurisdiction over the South, the claim to which was abandoned, before 1866, by unanimous vote, including Thompson's! It denies the legality of the Southern Supreme Council, from which alone the *Thirty-third* degree came, and which Thompson by his vote recognized and whose recognition and fraternal support, he, with his associates, sought to obtain."[27]

The visit to Europe of Henry J. Seymour referred to in the above quotation had serious consequences. We find that Seymour at that time was in communication with John Yarker with whom he collaborated in founding the Ancient and Primitive Rite, the ramifications of which reach to all the branches of occult illuminism such as Societas Rosicruciana in Anglia, Memphis and Mizraim, Ancient Order of Oriental Templars, etc.

CHAPTER LXV

CARBONARISM
(THE ALTA VENDITA) (HAUTE VENTE D'ITALIE)
(ALTA VENDITA [LODGE] FOUNDED 1809)

THE CARBONARI HAD existed internationally, it is said, under different names since the days of Francis I, King of France, but not till the year 1815 did we begin to hear of its individual historical achievements.

The following is a translation of one of the secret official documents published in Italy by the highest authority of the order, for the guidance of the active head-centres of Masonry in 1818, under the title of: *Permanent Instructions*, or *Practical Code of Rules; Guide for the Heads of the Highest Grades of Masonry.*[28] The original Italian document was given to Nubio, one of the Supreme Vendita (Alta Vendita) in 1824, when he was sent to Rome to carry it into effect, and it was to this instruction that he referred when he wrote from Forli to Signor Volpi: "As I have written to you before, I am appointed to demoralise the education of the youth of the Church". When these documents were lost, the Freemasons offered fabulous sums for their recovery. These secret *Instructions*, intended only for a chosen few Masons of heavy calibre, were written three years after what was called the "Restoration" of 1815, which was brought about by a number of veteran Freemasons, all born in the past century, who had preceded, made, planned, and passed through the French Revolution of 1789. They were rife with the republican notions of France and Italy.

They had survived their works, and had been in a great measure defeated, or at least modified, by Napoleon, in whose hands they were like a boat in the hands of new pilots, and, stunned by the many changes, were motionless for a time. In 1815, brought, as it were, in presence of a new world, they took breath and courage, and gathering up the broken threads of the tangled skein, determined to spend the rest of their lives in restoring, if possible, the web commenced in 1789 and 1783. The principal author was supposed to be a man of the name of Filippo Buonarotti, one of the great correspondents of Nubio. From his biography, given in the eighth volume of the *Mondo Segreto di Castro,* he would appear to have been an apt pupil and follower of Nubio's principle, *Ama nesciri et pro nihilo computari.* He was born at Pisa in 1761, was a friend of Robespierre, and an enemy of Napoleon, against whom he always conspired. He was a centre in Paris for both French and Italian Carbonari. He had been one of the principals in 1821,[29] and in 1830 founded the sect of the Apofesimeni. In a published record, entitled *Bologna of the New Secret Society,* 1835, we find the name of a young man, Giuseppe Petroni, afterwards a celebrated Mazzinian, and now (1878) Grand Master Aggunto of Roman Masonry of the Via della Valle, who was likewise one of this noble band. My readers may now thoroughly understand the character of the authors of this secret and curious document of the *Instructions.* It is a resume and summary, expressed in the clearest terms, of the aim of Freemasonry and the means by which it is attained; Freemasonry antecedent to the French Revolution; Freemasonry during the French Revolution; Freemasonry revived after the Restoration. Freemasonry, today, is one and the same, using the same means to work out the same end and object. "So these old conspirators of the past century wakened up in 1815 from their long sleep more energetic than ever, and as a first step towards reviving their secret society work, wrote the following *Permanent Instructions,* as a guide for the Higher initiated who were chosen to command the whole Masonic movement, especially in Italy:—

"Now that we are constituted in an active body, and that our Order begins to reign as well in places most remote as in those that are nearest our centre, one great thought arises, a thought that has always greatly preoccupied the men who aspire to the universal regeneration of the world, that thought is, the Liberation of Italy, for from Italy shall one day issue the freedom of the entire world—a Republic of Fraternity, Harmony, and Humanity. This great idea is not yet comprehended by our brothers of France. They believe that revolutionary Italy can only plot in the shade, and accomplish the stabbing of a few spies, or traitors, meantime bearing patiently the yoke of facts accomplished elsewhere, for Italy, but without Italy. This error has been very fatal to us. It is useless to combat it with words which would only propagate more. It is necessary to annihilate it with facts. And in the midst of anxieties, which agitate the most vigorous spirits of our society, one there is that can never be forgotten. The Papacy ever exercises a decisive influence over the lot of Italy. With the arm, the voice, the pen, of its innumerable bishops, monks, nuns, and faithful of all latitudes, the Pope finds everywhere persons enthusiastically prepared for sacrifice, and even for martyrdom, friends who would die for him, or sacrifice all for his love. It is a mighty lever, the full power of which few Popes understood, and which has as yet been used but partially. The question of today is not the reconstruction of a momentarily weakened power.

"Our final aim is that of Voltaire and of the French Revolution,— the complete annihilation of Catholicism, and ultimately of Christianity. Were Christianity to survive, even upon the ruins of Rome, it would, a little later on, revive and live. We must now consider how to reach our end, with certainty, not cheating ourselves with delusions, which would prolong indefinitely, and probably compromise, the ultimate success of our cause." Hearken not to those boastful and vainglorious French, and thick headed Germans, and hypochondriacal Englishmen, who seem to think it possible to end Catholicism, at one time by an obscene song, at another by an absurd sophism, and again by a contemptible sarcasm. Catholicism has a vitality which survives such attacks with ease. She has seen adversaries more implacable and more terrible far, and sometimes has taken a malicious pleasure in baptising with holy water the most rabid amongst them. We may therefore allow our brethren in those countries to work off their frenzy of anti-catholic zeal, allow them to ridicule our

Madonnas and our apparent devotion. Under this cloak, we may conspire at our convenience, and arrive, little by little, at our ultimate aim.

"Therefore, the Papacy has been for seventeen hundred years interwoven with the history of Italy. Italy can neither breathe nor move without the leave of the Supreme Pontiff. With him, she has the hundred arms of Briareus; without him, she is condemned to a lamentable impotency, and to divisions and hostility, from the foot of the Alps to the last pass of the Appennines. Such a state of things must not remain. It is necessary to seek a remedy. Very well. The remedy is at hand. The Pope, whoever he may be, will never enter into a secret society. It then becomes the duty of the Secret Society to make the first advance to the Church and to the Pope, with the object of conquering both. The work for which we gird ourselves up, is not the work of a day, nor of a month, nor of a year.

"It may last for many years, perhaps for a century; in our ranks the soldier dies, but the war is continued. We do not at present intend to gain the Pope to our cause, nor to make him a neophyte to our principles, or a propagator of our ideas. Such would be an insane dream. Even should it happen that any Cardinal, or any Prelate, of his own will, or by deception, should share in our secrets, such would not be a reason for desiring his exaltation to the Chair of Peter. Nay, his very exaltation would be our ruin; for this reason that, his apostasy being prompted by his ambition alone, that very ambition of power would necessarily impel him to sacrifice us.

"Catholics! what must we consider Freemasonry, when Freemasons themselves pronounce it an apostasy from Catholicity, and foresee that a powerfully acquainted with them and their machinations would, as a consequence, seek to crush them.

"That which we should seek, that which we should await, as the Jews await a Messiah, is a Pope according to our wants. An Alexander VI would not suit us, for he never erred in religious doctrine; a Pope Borgia would not suit us, for he was excommunicated by all the thinking philosophers and unbelievers for the vigour with which he defended the Church. We require a Pope for ourselves, if such a Pope were possible. With such a one we should march more securely to the storming of the Church than with all the little books of our French and English brothers.

"And why? Because it were useless to seek with these alone to split the rock upon which God has built his Church. We should not want the vinegar of Hannibal, nor gunpowder, nor even our arms, if we had but the little finger of the successor of Peter engaged in the plot; that little finger would avail us more for our crusade than all the Urbans II and St. Bernards for the crusade of Christianity. We trust that we may yet attain this supreme object of our efforts.

"But when? and how? The unknown cannot yet be seen. Nevertheless, as nothing should move us from our mapped-out plan, we must labour at our newly-commenced work as if tomorrow were to crown it with success. We wish, in this Instruction, which should be kept concealed from those simply initiated, to give advice to the rulers of the Supreme Vendita, which they, in turn, should inculcate in the brethren by means of *Insegnamento*, or Memorandum." Little can be done with old Cardinals and with prelates of decided character. Such incorrigibles must be left to the school of Gonsalvi, and in our magazines of popularity and unpopularity, we must find the means to utilize, or ridicule, power in their hands. A well invented report must be spread with tact amongst good Christian families: such a Cardinal, for instance, is a miser: such a prelate is licentious; such an official is a freethinker, an infidel, a Freemason, and so on in the same strain. These things will spread quickly to the cafes, thence to the squares, and one report is sometimes enough to ruin a man.

"If a prelate, or bishop, arrive in a province from Rome, to celebrate or officiate at some public function, it is necessary at once to become acquainted with his character, his antecedents, his temperament, his defects—especially his defects. If he should be our enemy—an Albani, a Pallotta, a Bernetti, a Delia Genga, a Rivarola—at once trap him, entangle him in all the nets and snares you can. Give him a character which must horrify the young people and the women; describe him as cruel, heartless, and bloodthirsty; relate some atrocious transaction which will easily cause a sensation amongst the people. The foreign newspapers will learn and copy these facts, which they will know how to embellish and colour according to their usual style.

"For respect due to truth show, or better still, quote from some respectable fool as having quoted the number of the journal which has given the names, acts and doings of these personages. As in England and in France, so also in Italy there will be no lack of writers who well know how to tell lies for the good cause, and have no difficulty in doing so. One newspaper publishing the name of a Monsignor Delegate, His Excellency, or Eminence, or Lord Justice, will be quite sufficient proof for the people; they will require no other. The people here around us in Italy are in the infancy of Liberalism. At present they believe in the Liberals, after a little they will believe in anything."

Modern Carbonarism was founded in 1815 by Maghella, a native of Genoa, who, at the time when Joachim Murat became King of the two Sicilies, was a subordinate of Saliceti, the Neapolitan Minister of Police. He was a Freemason, who exempted from initiation and probation all Freemasons who desired to become Carbonari. Anyone who has read the statutes and ritual of Carbonarism will see that it is one and the same as that of Masonry.[30]

A sequence of events pertaining to Carbonarism can be traced by the perusal of several works from which we quote:

At a meeting held on Oct. 13th 1820 by the Grand Secret Consistory, the Orient of Scotland was recognized. The two Consistories of Masonry in France and in Italy and that of the Sublime Carbonari were put into communication and their co-operation assured.[31]

The high ruling grades of the Carbonari appear to have been those of *Sublime Maître Parfait*, above which was still another that of the *Sublime Elus*.[32]

The Alta Vendita constituted the Supreme Directory of the Carbonari and was led by a group of Italian noblemen, amongst whom a prince, "the profoundest of initiates, was charged as Inspector General of the Order."

Piccolo Tigre, a certain nondescript Jew, rushed about Europe obeying orders and presumably giving them, but what he actually did has remained a mystery.

Giuseppe Mazzini had been initiated Carbonaro in 1827.[33] Sometime after, Carbonarism combined, or rather coalesced, with the Society known as Young Italy led by Mazzini whose aims were identical with those of the Carbonari.

Young Italy, Young Poland, Young England, Young Switzerland, Young Ireland—all together *Young Europe*—all international movements of the same character working towards the same end, viz. the supremacy of the Masters.

The Guelphic Knights, whose object was the independence of Italy, to be effected by means of all the secret societies of the country under their leadership, found able helpers in the Carbonari.

"The Chiefs of the Carbonari were also chiefs among the Guelphs; but only those that had distinct offices among the Carbonari could be admitted among the Guelphs. There can be no doubt that the Carbonari when the sect had become very numerous, partly sheltered themselves under the designation of Guelphs and Adelphi or Independents, by affiliating themselves to these societies."[34]

At one time the support of the Carbonari was offered by Maghella to Murat with the advice to declare against Napoleon and to proclaim the independence of Italy but Murat's subsequent proscription of the sect induced it to seek the support of England. The Bourbons and Lord William Bentinck favoured it while Murat ordered its extermination. Some of its leaders indeed perished but shortly afterwards the society was reorganized and a schismatic sect calling itself *Calderari* (Braziers) came into being.[35]

For the root of this movement see Chapter LIII.

For the development of this movement see Chapters LXX, LXXI, XCIII.

CHAPTER LXVI

THE MANCHESTER UNITY OF ODDFELLOWS ENGLAND
(FOUNDED 1810)

WE FIND THE following in the article on Oddfellows, in *Hastings' Encyclopaedia of Religions and Ethics*. "R. W. Moffrey (*Century* p. 18) fixes the year 1810 as that in which the Manchester Unity of Oddfellows started, though it was not till 1814 that the minutes of its Grand Committees began to be printed... however Spry (*Hist. of Oddfellowship* p. 16) gives minutes of a meeting of a 'lodge' No. 9, of the Order of Oddfellows, dated 12th March 1748, from which it would seem that eight previous lodges had been established before that date."

For the connection of this order with Freemasonry see Chapter XXVIII.

We also note the following:—

"The position of Friendly Societies generally before the introduction of National Insurance is shown in the report of the Chief Registrar of Friendly Societies for the year ending 31st December 1906 (*Parliamentary Papers of Session* 1907, n° 49, xi pp. 16–18)."

According to this report, we find that the order had 1,035,785 members and the income of the benefit funds was £1,703,674.

The Oddfellows resisted any proposal of State control or State interference with the working of Friendly Societies.

The English Order has four degrees.

CHAPTER LXVII

THE HETAIRIA OF GREECE
(ETHERISTS) (FOUNDED 1814)

HETAIRIA WAS THE Greek name for societies, organizations or associations. In ancient Greece the name *hetairia* applied to companies in the army. In more modern times, it was used for societies of learning, or commercial purposes and also for political secret societies.

It is in connection with the latter that we are concerned. While Greece was under Turkish dominion, the national aspirations of its people could be vented in secret only. The breath of revolution which swept Europe during the latter part of the 18th century stirred some of the Greek patriots whose aims was the overthrow of the Turkish power. The main leader at that time was Constantin Rhygas (1754–1798).

He formed the first secret societies of *Hetairias* which were mainly composed of Klephtes or bandits. Bound by oath, each member of the society was to use all means, assassination included, to free Greece. The execution of Rhygas drove the *hetairias* to seek cover but in 1814, a chief lodge was re-formed in Odessa under the name of *Hetairia phileke*. Its avowed aim was the liberation of Greece, and its main seat was in Russia. Every candidate took an oath, as in all secret societies, and knew no one beyond his initiator and sponsor. Funds, collected and administered by a superior council directing all the lodges, were kept in Russia.

When a sufficient number of *Hetairias* were organized and a chief needed to direct the movement against Turkey, Count Capo d'Istria, (John, 1776–1831) a Greek, minister in Russia under the Tzar Alexander I, and author of the text of the Holy Alliance was asked to take the lead but refused, and Alexander Ypsilanti was nominated. The insurrection broke out in 1821.

Among the most prominent members of the *Hetairia* we find Alexander Mavrocordato (1791–1865) who was under the influence of England and was also the friend of Byron whom he had met in Missolonghi in 1822. From him he received funds for the purchase of arms to the extent of one hundred thousand francs. It is related that Lord Byron died in his arms at Missolonghi in 1824. Among the supporters of the London Branch of the Philhellenic Committee were Jeremy Bentham, Sir Francis Burdett, Lord Erskine, Lord Ebrington, Sir John Cam Hobhouse, (afterwards Lord Brougham) Joseph Hume, Sir James Mackintosh and Lord John Russell. These foreign committees provided arms, money and volunteers.

The following details concerning the organization of the *Hetairia* of Greece are set forth in *The Secret Societies of the European Revolution*, by Thomas Frost (Vol. II, page 47 et seq.).

"Less simple than that of the Carbonari, the system rather resembled that of the Illuminati in the number of grades and relation of the branch societies to each other."

There were five grades namely:—

- The Adelphoi (Brothers, who took an oath of secrecy but ignored the aims of the society),
- The Systemenoi (Bachelors, who knew that Greece was to be freed by revolution),
- The Priests of Eleusis,
- The Prelates (knowing all the secrets),
- The Grand Arch (The supreme directing control of 12 members).

"Early in 1827 a motion was unanimously adopted by the Senate favouring the placing of Greece under the protection of Great Britain."

This followed a secret interview of Mavrocordato with Sir Stratford Canning, but Mavrocordato retired from public life "on the failure of his project for the establishment of a constitutional kingdom under British protection."

"Hostilities in Greece were finally terminated, in the summer of 1828, by a convention concluded at Alexandria between Admiral Codrington and Mehemet Ali, by which the latter agreed to withdraw the Egyptian troops from the Morea."

The arbitrary government of Capo d'Istria ended on October 24, 1831, when he was assassinated.

CHAPTER LXVIII

THE HUNG SOCIETY OF CHINA
(FOUNDED ABOUT 1815)

THIS SOCIETY HAS also been known as The Triad Society, The Ghee Hon, The Society of Heaven and Earth (T'in Tei Hui), Ts'ing-lin-Kiu, The San-ho-hoei and the Sam-ho-hui.

After the Emperor Kang Hsi issued a Sacred Edict in 1662, ordering the suppression of Buddhism and Taoism in China, the Hung and the White Lotus, the latter a Taoist mystical society also known by the name "White Lily", are said to have united to fight the Manchu Dynasty as their common enemy.

They are supposed to have finally merged towards 1815 as a secret political occult organization.

In 1851 the Hung broke into open revolt against the Manchus. This is known as the Taiping Revolt and is often alluded to as "The Triad War". It was led by a village schoolmaster called Hung who, after his defeat by Gordon in 1864, committed suicide.

Since the Taiping revolt the Society has been less conspicuous but it is supposed nevertheless to have inspired the successful revolution which in 1911 overthrew the Manchu Dynasty and established the Republic of which Dr. Sun Yat-Sen assumed the presidency on January 1, 1912.

Dr. Sun Yat-Sen, nominally a Christian, was a member of the Hung Society, and his first official action as the first President of the Chinese

Republic was to enable Yuan Shi-Kai to unite all parties under his presidency. He then accepted for himself the Presidency of Nanking. The people received his proclamation announcing these changes in front of the Ming tombs, and listened while he told the spirits of the Mings that the Manchu despotism, having fallen, China was now a Republic.

The Hung[36] having been outlawed since 1890 in China as a terrorist organization, now, as a secret society, holds its meetings in the woods at night with the approaches well-guarded.

The English branch of this society is at Liverpool where it operates as a mutual benefit and charitable institution.

As the rights of citation from this book are withheld from the public we are unable to give quotations from it here, but we recommend the first twenty-two pages as of interest to historical students.

CHAPTER LXIX

RITE OF MEMPHIS
(FOUNDED 1815)

THIS RITE WAS founded in 1815 by Sam Honis (from Cairo), Gabriel Mathieu, Baron Dumas, Marquis de Laroque and Hippolite Labrunie.

The Grand Lodge Osiris in Paris was founded in 1839. Jacques Etienne Marconis was Grand Master.

In his *History of Freemasonry*, Freke-Gould states that "J. E. Marconis, Grand Hierophant, inaugurated the Rite in person at New York in 1857, and afterwards in 1862 chartered it as a Sovereign Sanctuary—by which body a charter was granted on Jan. 3rd, 1872, for another Sovereign Sanctuary in and for the British Islands whose officers were duly installed Oct. 8th in the same year."

The order is now known in England as "The Ancient and Primitive Rite."

On December 30, 1862, the rite of Memphis merged finally into the Grand Orient of France and in England, in 1875 under the name of Ancient and Primitive Rite, it amalgamated with that oi Mizraim which Gould informs us had no separate governing body in chat country.

In 1865, the Grand Orient reduced the original 97 degrees to 33.

A. E. Waite in *Devil Worship in France* outlines the later history of the rite in the following sentence:

"Garibaldi succeeded Jacques Etienne Marconis of Paris, becoming president of a confederation of the Rites which was brought about by Mr. John Yarker in the year 1881.[37]

CHAPTER LXX

THE CALDERARI
(FOUNDED 1816)

THE "CALDERARI DEL CONTRAPESO," an offshoot of the Carbonari, came into prominence about 1816.

Their first organizer, The Prince of Canosa, became Minister of Police under Ferdinand, King of Naples, in December, 1819.

The Calderari were the sworn enemies of the Freemasons and Carbonari.

They took the following oath:—

"I, N. N., promise and swear upon the Trinity, as supreme director of the universe, upon this cross, and upon this steel, the avenging instrument of the perjured—to live and die in the Roman Catholic and Apostolic faith, and to defend with my blood this religion, and the society of True Friendship, the Calderari, to which I am about to belong. I swear never to offend, in honour, life, or property, the children of True Friendship; I promise and swear to all the Knights, true friends, all possible succour that shall depend on me.

I swear to initiate no person into the Society before I arrive at the 4th rank. I swear eternal hatred to all Masonry, and to its atrocious protectors; as well as to all Jansenists, Materialists, Economists, and Illuminati. I swear, as I value my life, never to admit any of them into the Society of Friendship. Lastly, I swear, that if, through wickedness or levity, I suffer myself to commit perjury, I submit to the loss of life as the punishment of my error, and then to be burnt: and may my ashes, scattered to the wind, serve as an example to the children of Friendship throughout the whole world. And so help me God, for the happiness of my soul, and the repose of my conscience."[38]

For root of this movement see Chapter LXV.

For development of this movement see Chapter CXXVI.

CHAPTER LXXI

FRENCH CARBONARISM
(FOUNDED 1820)

THE MASONIC LODGE *Les Amis de la Verite* was founded in 1820 by Buchez, Flotard, Bazard and Joubert, all Freemasons, for political purposes. On a riot incited by members of this lodge a young man was killed. As a consequence of his death this lodge went out of existence.

One of its former members, Dugied, a Freemason, was initiated into the mysteries of Carbonarism while at Naples.[39] Having conceived the project of introducing this association into France he discussed the matter with another ex-member of the Ami's *de la Verite,* Flotard, and together they decided to put the idea into practice by taking as a nucleus of the new organization the remains of *Les Amis de la Verite.*

The society was organized as follows:—

The one "Haute Vente", central "Ventes" and individual "Ventes" (lodges).

The "Haute Vente" was the committee of direction and action. Two members of the committee having found an adept, the adept would agree with them to form a "Vente". The adept would become President one of the others censor, the other deputy, the role of the last being to keep in touch with the committee while allowing the president to believe that this committee was only a superior degree of the association; The censor's business was to inspect the work of the "Ventes". These three chiefs were then required to annex 17 recruits, thus bringing the number of a lodge up to twenty. Thus constituted, this group was called a central "Vente". Two of its members made below what had been made above them, forming an individual "Vente" of the first order, which, repeating the same process formed an ordinary individual "Vente" thus extending indefinitely the ramifications of the sect.

A similar organization, but under different names, was adapted to the army. There the Haute Vente was called the Legion, the central Ventes, the Cohortes, the individual Ventes of the first order the Centuries; and the ordinary individual Ventes the Manipules.

This double system was intended to puzzle the police, by making it believe that there was a separate association in the army. A further measure of precaution forbade a Carbonaro, under penalty of death, being affiliated to another Vente. This precaution was intended to prevent anyone entering different groups and thus possibly discovering and denouncing the secrets of the society.

The direction of the Ventes was indeed centralized but this unity of control was to be ignored by most of the members.

The Carbonari had no settled principles. It accepted all opinions provided these favoured the elimination of royal families. The imperialists and liberals formed important nuclei. The latter, the sons of middle-class parents, stirred against the government by patriotism, youth and class jealousy, dreamed only of grabbing the influence of the old families. As for what is called the people, it did not count in Carbonarism; the illustrious role attributed to it later had not yet been invented!

To begin with, the Haute Yente counted only seven members: Dugied, Flotard, Bazard, Buchez, Joubert, Carriol, Limperani. Among them we find again the four heads of the *Amis de la Vérité*.

The Carbonari having prospered, the Haute Vente found it advisable to annex some notable characters. Among others, the Freemason General Lafayette, who, even in old age, had a childish weakness for popularity, accepted the offer to join the conspiracy.

Towards the end of 1820 the society had many branches, notably those of Bordeaux, Nantes, Toulouse, La Bochelle, Poitiers, Colmar, Belfort, etc.

The subversive efforts of this society culminated in an abortive attempt at Revolution at La Bochelle, and the subsequent arrest of many of its principal members completed its nominal dissolution.

After the *debacle* at La Rochelle the *Amis de la Verite* merged into the Amis du Peuple which in turn, in 1832, became the *Droits de l'Homme*. After its unsuccessful attempt to assassinate the king, (Louis Philippe) in 1835 the remains of the *Droits de l'Homme* reorganized as the *Societe des Families* with Blanqui and Barbes as leaders. According to Lucien de la Hodde,[40] Carbonarism in France had ceased to exist by 1822, except for a few obstinates like Charles Teste, (a friend of Babeuf) and Buonarotti who remained faithful to the old organization. Lucien de la Hodde however, while following Carbonarism, lost sight of the Haute Vente which, working through Mazzini and the International Committee of London, directed its work of destruction in France through Ledru Rollin and Felix Pyat. After its collapse in 1836 the *Société des Families* became that of the *Saisons* (seasons) and it was a branch of this society, the *Société dissidents*, that served the purpose of the Haute Vente in 1848 by aiding in the terrorisation of Paris and the fall of the Monarchy.

The self-appointed members of the provisional government of France after the abdication of the king were:—Dupont (de l'Eure) Member of the original Carbonari founded in 1820, Arago, Lamartine, Ledru Rollin, Garnier-Pagès, Marie, and Cremieux.

Lucien de la Hodde was the agent of the French Secret Police, and for 8 years before the revolution of 1848 occupied an exalted position in the ranks of the Revolutionaries.

His conclusions are strangely at variance with the facts which he relates. On page 381, he tells how an indiscretion on the part of Caussidière, one of his associates, placed the blame of a conspiracy upon Ledru Rollin and, because Ledru Rollin calmly denied knowledge of the affair, de la Hodde accepts his statement without question.

Though a bona-fide student of the subject, it is quite evident that de la Hodde had failed to grasp the principle upon which Revolutionary organizations operate, viz: that of a body of dupes whose particular job is genuinely to believe that their organization is the executive one. Into this one all persons of doubtful revolutionary integrity are steered, and, in this branch of the machine, conscientiously attend to their business, while the real agents do their savage work.

For root of movement see Chapter LXV.

For development of movement see Chapters LXXXV, XCIII.

CHAPTER LXXII

MODERN KNIGHTS TEMPLAR
(POLAND) (FOUNDED 1822)

HECKETHORN[41] TELLS US of a sect which arose in Poland in 1818 which he refers to as that of "National Freemasonry", which borrowed the rites, degrees, and language of Freemasonry, but aimed at national independence. The society was open to persons of all classes, but sought chiefly to enlist soldiers and officials, so as to turn their technical knowledge to account in the day of the struggle. But though numerous, the society lasted only a few years: for disunion arose among the members, and it escaped total dissolution only by transformation. It altered its rites and ceremonies, and henceforth called itself the "Scythers", in remembrance of the revolution of 1794, in which whole regiments, armed with scythes, had gone into battle.

They met in 1821 at Warsaw, and drew up a new revolutionary scheme, adopting at the same time the new denomination of "Patriotic Society". In the meanwhile, the students of the university of Wilna had formed themselves into a secret society which, however, was discovered by the Russian government and dissolved. In 1822, the Patriotic Society combined with the masonic rite of "Modern Templars", founded in Poland by Captain Maiewski; to the three rites of symbolical masonry was added a fourth, in which the initiated swore to do all in his power towards the liberation of his country. These combined societies brought about the insurrection of 1830. In 1834 was established the society of "Young Poland" by Simon Konarski.

Simon Konarski (1808–1839) was a young Polish patriot and poet, one of the most active members of the Young Poland movement founded by Joseph Mazzini in 1834. He travelled to France, England and Belgium and, in the latter country, namely in Brussels, was in constant touch with Lelewel who had been chosen by Mazzini to become the link between himself and the Polish revolutionists. In Paris, the Young Poland movement was directed by Zwierkowsky.

Simon Konarski was seized by the Russian authorities and executed in 1839 at Wilna.

CHAPTER LXXIII

THE ST. PATRICK BOYS
(FOUNDED 1825)

AS REGARDS THIS organization, Pollard writes "In 1825 the name of the Ribbon men was changed officially to the *St. Patrick's Fraternal Organization*, otherwise known as the *St. Patrick's Boys*. This change was essential as, like their predecessors the White Boys,[42] the eminently Catholic Association of Ribbon men had now been excommunicated by the Catholic Church."[43]

CHAPTER LXXIV

BRAHMO SOMAJ
(FOUNDED 1830)

THE BRAHMO SOMAJ movement, also called Brahmoism or Brahmaism, was founded by Rajah Ram Mohun Roy (1774–1833), in 1830.

Its main object was to fight idolatrous rites and practices, and, by many, it has been described as a "Hindu Unitarian Church."

The chief achievement of Ram Mohun Roy was the abolition by Lord William Bentinck of the practice of "suttee" (sacrifice of the widow on the funeral pyre of her husband).

Ram Mohun Roy's principles were Theistic. He had also for several years studied Lamaism in the Himalayas. Having come to England in 1830, he was received with much honour by many sections of society and entertained by Louis Philippe. He was considered a great authority by all those who at that time were conducting spiritualist and psychic researches. He died at Bristol.

A great impulse was given to the Brahmo Somaj by Debendra Nath Tagore (also written Devendranath Takur) who had joined it in 1842 and is considered as its second founder.

Owing to his efforts, the institution became purely Theistic, giving up the authority of the Yedas and eliminating the Vedantic element from the Brahmic covenant. In 1856, Debendra Nath Tagore had also gone to the Himalayas where he spent three years as a disciple of the Tibetan

Lamas. Later, he was joined in his work by his friend Keshub Chunder Sen who, however, in 1863, devoured by the ambition of becoming sole leader, attacked the Somaj, heading what one might call the revolt of the "Young Brahmaists" and with his followers seceded from the Mother organization.

The schism gave rise to the formation of another Somaj which was directed by Keshub Chunder Sen under the name Somaj of India, whereas the former organization, remaining under the leadership of Debendra Nath Tagore, was called Adi Samaj or Original Church. It was also named "Conservative", in opposition to the new institution termed "Progressive".

Keshub Chunder Sen retained power in his organization; the foundation stone of the Somaj of India Church was laid at Jhamapukur in Calcutta, in 1868. In 1870 he journeyed to England where he was enthusiastically received by the spiritualist centres of the day, and succeeded in exciting much interest in the political, social and religious affairs of India. In 1878, his disregard for the rules of the Somaj regarding Hindu marriages which he infringed in the matter of the wedding of his own daughter to the young Maharajah of Kuch Behar, caused another split in the ranks of the Somaj of India. The dissidents then formed the Sadharan Brahmo Somaj.

The career of Keshub Chunder Sen must be followed with interest by students of Theosophy. Therein will they find many of the odd principles and injunctions laid down by H. P. Blavatsky and Annie Besant. For instance, the theocratic system was that promoted by Keshub Chunder Sen in his efforts to found a universal religion which would unite all creeds and symbols; the Christian Cross, the Crescent, the Vedic Om, the Saiva's trident and the Vaishnava's Khunti. By means of imaginary pilgrimages, he led his adherents successively to the shrines of Moses, Buddha, to the Himalayan heights and Lama teachers, to Jesus and to Mahomet.

Similarly to Annie Besant's Khrishnamurti, he allowed himself to be worshipped as the *Saviour of Sinners*; his theory was the reincarnation of Great Men of which he was one. Further, he complacently allowed his followers to raise him to the dignity of a deity. As the Kheshub Chunder

Sen's worship increased, there grew also the dogma of Divine Injunction. A salient feature of Keshub's teaching was the belief or blind faith in the revelations claimed to have been made to invisible teachers and spiritual guides and exaction of blind obedience to their commands. We are forcibly reminded of the claim made by H. P. Blavatsky to her followers to sign their blind acceptance of all orders presumably received from invisible masters like her Koot Hoomi.

Another feature which, later, distinguished Keshub Chunder Sen's devotees was the "Bhakti" side of their religion. Unlike "Yoga", the old Hindu type of religious meditation or contemplation, "Bhakti", which has been chiefly developed by the followers of Chaytania in India, is a manifestation of religious frenzy. It spurns the aspiration to approach God by concentration of thought and desire as well as silent communion, which they deem unprofitable and vain. The philosophy of "Bhakti" is that the love of God must be strong to the point of being maddening. It therefore induces dancing, sobbing, swooning. The more frenzied the manifestations, the greater the religious perfection. A great Bhakta is one who, like the founder of the school, shows the greatest religious madness.

Women devotees of Keshub Chunder Sen's following were formed into a sisterhood in 1881 and one hears of "ladies' journeys to the Spirit land". The readers of "Inquire Within"[44] will remember the description of "journeys in the Astral" claimed to have been accomplished by women adepts of the Stella Matutina Order. Soon after, also in 1881, young men were likewise formed into a brotherhood and were initiated into different holy orders. In both cases, the number of initiates was 11. The ceremony of initiation was called New Horn, Sacred Fire or Blazing Agni. Most of the rites are found in the different branches of Theosophy and Anthroposophy, all centered around this sacred fire also named Kundalini.

In 1880, Keshub Chunder Sen had given his organization another name, that of "The New Dispensation".

It is in the *Societas Rosicruciana in Anglia* that one must seek the amalgamation of Jewish Cabala magic and Hindu magic. The latter swept over Europe with the spread of Theosophy and flourished particularly in

England. There it had found a ground in 1830 with the teachings given by Ram Mohun Roy to the spiritualists of that day with whom he had formed a Brahmo Somaj circle.

For root of this movement see Chapter XIV.

For development of this movement see Chapters CX and CXXI.

CHAPTER LXXV

THE MORMONS
(FOUNDED 1830)

SOON AFTER THE establishment of Mormonism its founder, Joseph Smith, conceived the idea of establishing a Masonic super rite.

In M. R. Werner's book *Brigham Young* (page 62) the following remark makes this evident.

"Masonry was always popular with the Mormons until Joseph Smith claimed that an angel of the Lord had brought him the lost key-words of several degrees, enabling him to progress further than the highest Masons. The charter of the Mormon lodge was then taken away by the Grand Lodge".

Joseph Smith, applying his powers of mediumship towards the realization of the ambitious project nurtured by General Pepe, Mazzini and others for the establishment of a super rite, was not necessarily acceptable to the Masonic leaders of his time.

Thus as a Mason he failed but as the founder of a Masonic sect he succeeded.

So much has already been written about the sect of the Mormons that we confine ourselves here to a short sketch of opinion and descriptions given by various authors. The following is extracted from *The Encyclopaedia Britannica*, 9th Edition.

"This is a religious non-Christian sect, founded by Joseph Smith at Manchester, New York, in 1830, now settled in Salt Lake City, Territory of Utah, United States... Smith was born Dec. 23rd, 1805, at Sharon, Windsor County, Vermont, from which place ten years later his parents, a poor, ignorant, thriftless, and not too honest couple, removed to New York, where they settled on a small farm near Palmyra, Wayne County (then Ontario). Four years later, in 1809, they removed to Manchester, some six miles off; and it was at the latter place when fifteen years old that Joseph began to have his alleged visions, in one of which on the night of 21st Sept., 1823, the angel Moroni appeared to him three times, and told him that the Bible of the Western Continent, the supplement to the New Testament, was buried in a certain spot near Manchester. Thither, four years later and after due disciplinary probation, Smith went, and had delivered into his charge by an angel of the Lord a stone box, in which was a volume, 6 inches thick, made of thin gold plates 8 inches by 7, and fastened together by three gold rings. The plates were covered with small writing in the 'reformed Egyptian' tongue, and were accompanied by a pair of supernatural spectacles, consisting of two crystals set in a silver bow, and called 'Urim and Thummim'; by aid of these, the mystic characters could be read. Being himself unable to read or write fluently, Smith employed as amanuensis one Oliver Cowdery, to whom from behind a curtain, he dictated a translation, which, with the aid of a farmer, Martin Harris,[45] who had more money than wit, was printed and published in 1830 under the title of *The Book of Mormon* and accompanied by the sworn statement of Oliver Cowdery, David Whitmer, and Martin Harris, that an angel of God had shown them the plates of which the book was a translation. This testimony all three, on renouncing Mormonism some years later, denounced as false; but meanwhile it helped Smith to impose on the credulous, particularly in the absence of the gold plates themselves which suddenly and mysteriously disappeared."

Blanchard draws a parallel between this story of the gold plates and that of the legend of the 14th degree of Scottish Rites Masonry, that of Grand Elect Perfect and Sublime Mason, according to which "the real name of God was lost, till it was found by Masons, engraved on a three-cornered gold plate, in "the ruins of Enoch."[46]

In reality, this book "was written in 1812 as an historical romance by one Solomon Spalding, a crackbrained preacher; and the MS. falling into the hands of an unscrupulous compositor, Sidney Rigdon, was copied by him, and subsequently given to Joseph Smith. Armed with this book and with self-assumed divine authority, the latter soon began to attract followers."[47]

Joseph Smith was a Mason.

The Gold Plate trick, having worked so successfully once, was tried again in 1843 when six plates were found by Robert Wiley, a merchant of Kinderhook, Illinois. "The true story of the plates was disclosed" so Stuart Martin writes in *The Mystery of Mormonism* (page 69), in an affidavit made by W. Fulgate, of Mount Station, Brown County, Ill. on June 30th, 1879, when he swore before J. Brown, Justice of the Peace, that the "plates were humbug, gotten up by Robert Wiley, Bridge Whitton, and myself. Whitton, who was a blacksmith, cut the plates out of pieces of copper. Wiley and I made the hieroglyphics by making impressions of beeswax and filling them with acid." He describes the burial and the finding of the plates, and states that among the spectators at the "discovery" were two Mormon Elders, Marsh and Sharp.

Smith and his followers founded the city of Nauvoo and "such were the powers granted them by this charter as to render the city practically independent of the State Government, and to give Smith all but unlimited civil power. He organized a military body called the Nauvoo legion, of which he constituted himself commander with the title of lieutenant-general, while he was also president of the church and mayor of the city. On April 6th, 1841, the foundations of the new temple were laid, and the city continued to grow rapidly in prosperity and size."

Smith's career of treason, profligacy, dishonesty, polygamy, spiritism and humbug, came to an abrupt end when the gaol in which he was imprisoned by order of the Governor of the State was broken into by a mob who shot him and his fellow prisoner, his brother Hyram.

As head of the Mormons he was succeeded by Brigham Young (1801–1877).

In 1846, the repeal by the legislature of the charter of Nauvoo resulted in the Mormons being driven from the city.

In March 1849, they held a convention at Salt Lake City, and a State was organized under the name of "Deseret". "A legislature was elected and a constitution framed, which was sent on to Washington. This, Congress refused to recognize, and by way of compromise for declining to admit the proposed new State into the Union, President Fillmore in 1850 organized the country occupied by the Mormons into the Territory of Utah, with Brigham Young as governor." Adopting Smith's policy of aggressive military action, Brigham Young, like his predecessor, defied the Federal Government. He died on August 29, 1877, leaving 17 wives and 56 children.[48]

The following description of a Mormon ceremony was printed in the Rosicrucian in an article entitled "Ancient and Modern Mysteries" by M. W. Frater Robert Wentworth Little (page 169).

"The converts are then required to purchase white linen garments, which are furnished by the 'high deacon'. They are then conducted to the temple, ushered into a private room, and commanded to undress for the inspection of the presiding elder. This official, after a minute examination, clothes the neophytes in the linen robes or garments of endowment and conducts them into a large room which is divided by white screens into many small compartments. Each neophyte enters one of the compartments, and is ordered to take off the 'endowment robe' and to step into a long coffin shaped tin bath. The elder then pours water upon the naked victim—blessing each member of the body as the water touches it—'the brain to be clear and strong—the eyes to be bright and sharp—the ears to be quick to hear', and so on down to the feet—this ceremony being performed upon all, without distinction of sex. A new name is then given to each convert by the elder, who commands them to 'arise and follow me'. A magnificent garden, full of exquisite fruit trees, is the scene of the next ceremony. The candidates are still in a state of nudity, which represents primeval innocence, and the Temptation of our First Parents is the subject

of the next drama. The women are directed by an elder personating Satan
to pluck an apple from a certain tree, and after they have tasted, to hand
it to the men. Brigham Young then appears, and drives them out of the
garden with a flaming sword. They return to the temple, implore forgive-
ness on their knees for all trespasses and transgressions and the ceremony
concludes with a benediction upon the new Saints, pronounced by the
lips of this polygamous president. "Such is a brief outline of the 'Rite of
Endowment' the details of the scene being, as may readily be conceived,
of too obscene a character to be explained at greater length."

Brigham Young was succeeded by John Taylor, an Englishman and
a Freemason. His apostolic successors were Wilford Woodruff, Lorenzo
Snow, Joseph Fielding Smith (eldest son of the founder of the order) who
died Nov. 19th, 1918, and Heber J. Grant.[49]

About Mormonism and Masonry, Blanchard makes the following
remark: "The two institutions are morally and legally the same."[50]

The Mormon dogma is universality, materialism and pantheism. It
blends Judaism and Christianity, aiming at a progressive universal religion
while seeking to unite in itself all faiths and the cults of every people on
earth.

The Mormon state is a theocratic community at the head of which is
a grand priest-president assisted by two others and a travelling council of
twelve. Its mysteries are those of spiritism and the séance room.

For root of this movement see Chapter XLVII.

CHAPTER LXXVI

INDEPENDENT ORDER O F B'NAI B'RITH
(I. O. B. B.) (JEWISH MASONRY)
(FOUNDED 1843)

B'NAI B'RITH MEANS "Sons of the Covenant", the Covenant being that of circumcision practised according to the Mosaic law. Hence the Independent Order of the B'nai B'rith admits only Jews as members.

This rite "was founded in New York in 1843 by a number of German Jews, headed by Henry Jones."[51]

Its constitution, District Lodges, Grand Lodges, stamp it as a Jewish Masonic Society.

Like most societies, it covers its political activities under the cloak of "benevolence and philanthropy." From its inception until the present time, its main contact has been with Germany and its chief aim the establishment of the supremacy of the German Jews in all world affairs through the channel of "Internationalism". In 1882, the strength of the I. 0. B. B. in the United States warranted the opening of Lodges in Germany by Moritz Ettinger, and the growth of the order was so rapid there that in 1885, Julius Bien, President of the Order in New York, went over and inaugurated the first German Grand Lodge of the I. O. B. B.

The political activities of the leaders of the order in Bumania, Austria and Hungary are a matter of record, although the chief centre of their power is in the United States where they have lately attained supremacy in the Jewish World by absorbing "national" Zionism and submitting it wholly to their own "international" policy when the Jewish World Agency was created in October, 1928.

It will be well for the reader to bear in mind that, however united a front the Jews may present to the Gentiles, yet among themselves they are divided, and the fight for supremacy and the attainment of world power is not less bitter between their various camps than it is among the different sects of Freemasonry.

Rabbi Dr. Leo Bach was the president of the B'nai B'rith of Germany in 1928.

The Grand Master for Russia of the International Order of the B'nai B'rith at the time of the Russian revolution of 1917 was Sliozberg. He was one of the inspirers of Kerensky, the leader of the first revolution of 1917.[52] Alexander Kerensky, real name Aron Kirbiz, Kerensky having been the name of his stepfather, was a member of the Socialist revolutionary party and a 32nd degree Scottish Bites Mason.

There is but little doubt now that the B'nai B'rith seems to be the supreme body, shaping and directing, for the attainment of its own ends, the policies, whatever they may be, of all Freemasonry beginning with the Grand Lodge of England, The Grand Orient and Scottish Bites, and ending in the O. T. O., which is Illuminism under another name.

For root of this movement see Chapter VII.

For development of this movement see Chapter CXXVII.

CHAPTER LXXVII

YOUNG IRELAND
(FOUNDED 1843)

CAPTAIN H. B. C. Pollard, in writing of the Young Ireland movement says "The leaders of the Young Ireland Party of 1848 were John Mitchell, an advanced Radical, deeply tinged with Jacobin ideas, and William Smith O'Brien, whose brother later became Lord Inchiquin. They obtained popular support by reason of the widespread misery caused by the Potato famine of 'Black Forty-seven.' Gavan Duffy, Dillon, Doheny, O'Gorman and Stephens were all minor conspirators. Mitchell and O'Brien were transported to Van Diemens Land, but the younger men mostly made good their escape and lived in exile in Paris and America."[53]

"The old traditional combination of an open movement within the law reinforced by a secret organization of criminal habits was revived in 1850, when the *Tenant Defence Society* was founded with the object of enforcing, by agitation, legislation which was to accomplish by legal means that expropriation of property that the combined genius of White-feet, Rockites, Tenvalts, Molly Maguires and all other Irish terrorist societies had failed to achieve by violence."[54] The Archbishop of Dublin at that time was Archbishop Cullen, who was familiar with the evils resulting from the effective use of Secret Societies. He had been in Rome when the successful Carbonarists under Mazzini and Garibaldi drove out the Pope;[55] and the lesson had not been wasted. Cullen readily ascertained that the *Tenants' Rights Party* was merely a new disguise for the late 'Young Ireland' movement, whose ideals were both Republican and, within limits, anti-clerical.

"There was no formal excommunication, but a quiet though firm ban was placed on the party."[56]

The Young Ireland Movement was but a branch of the Young Europe Movement led by Mazzini, the main history of which will be found in Part I.

For root of this movement see Chapters LXIII, LXV.

For development of this movement see Chapter LXXXII.

CHAPTER LXXVIII

THE BAHAI MOVEMENT
(FOUNDED 1844)

"INQUIRE WITHIN", IN her book *Light-bearers of Darkness*, gives an excellent summary of the origin and scope of this sect. From her work we quote the following: "This movement was founded in 1844 by a Persian, Mirza Ali Muhammad, who took the title of 'Bab' (the Gate); he revolted against the Hierarchy, who, fearing his growing influence, had him shot at Tabriz, 1850.

"It claims to be the fulfilment 'of that which was but partially revealed in previous dispensations', and they look upon Buddha, Zoroaster, Jesus, Mohammed, and Confucius as merely preparing the world for the advent of the 'Most Great Peace' and the 'Mighty World Educator' Baha'u'llah (Glory of God), 1863–92, and later Abdul-Baha, 1892–1921. It further claims to be the unity of all religions, also older and modern movements, such as Theosophy, Freemasonry, Spiritualism, Socialism, etc.; it aims at conferring illumination upon humanity, and like all illuminated groups, it works for universal peace, religion, education, language (Esperanto), and universal everything leading to unity of humanity; therefore all prejudices must be abandoned, traditional, racial, patriotic, religious and political; all religions must be in accordance with science and reason."

The Bahais have a temple in Chicago, the building of which was begun in 1903 which "Inquire Within" describes as being a perfect nonagon in form, all its dimensions being based on the number nine, "the cabalistic number of generation, which initiates and leads to unity with the universal astral light."[57]

The same author further explains the organization of the sect most concisely in the following lines:

"There is a Guardian of the Cause—Shogi-Effendi—with nine co-workers, and in each town there is a Spiritual Assembly of nine members, who must be consulted, absolutely obeyed, and submitted to. There are also National Spiritual Assemblies in all countries to which the cause has spread, and, finally, they are making elaborate plans to form an International Spiritual Assembly to be elected by all believers—to enact ordinances and regulations not found in the explicit Holy Text."

We leave it to anyone interested to follow the subversive activities of this sect in either the political or religious realm.

For root of this movement see Chapter IV.

CHAPTER LXXIX

THE INDEPENDENT ORDER OF ODDFELLOWS
(I. O. O. F.) (AMERICAN)
(FOUNDED 1844)

THE FOLLOWING INFORMATION is gathered from *The Complete Manual of Oddfellows.*

"In 1819, Thomas Wildey established in Baltimore the first lodge of Oddfellows in the United States, and from 1825 till 1833, he was Grand Sire of the Grand Lodge.

"In 1843 Grand Sire Howell Hopkins of Pennsylvania was installed, and the United States Grand Lodge issued a dispensation for opening the Prince of Wales Lodge No. 1 at Montreal, Canada.

"In 1844 The Grand Lodge (Oddfellows U. S. A.) appointed a Ritual Revision Committee and entirely changed all the working, rejecting the whole of the English work, and in point of fact creating an entirely new Order"[58] based on the plans of Thomas Wildey. (See part I of this book).

The woman's degree of "Rebeckah", which was formulated by Schuyler Colfax in 1851, was adopted by the Grand Lodge in September of that year.[59]

The American Oddfellows have five degrees.

CHAPTER LXXX

MODERN SPIRITISM
(FOUNDED 1848)

MODERN SPIRITISM, SOMETIMES called Spiritualism, traces its descent from the mystifications of Catherine and Margaret Fox, the daughters of John Fox, who, in 1848, during the course of experiments conducted in a haunted house at Hydesville, New York, U. S. A. elaborated a system of communication by raps, with invisible entities. Both sisters eventually confessed to having abused the credulity of the public in their spiritist séances but the universal interest aroused by the phenomena at Hydesville did not abate.

Since then, there has been a regular epidemic of table turning, ouija boards, planchettes, automatic writings and similar modes, more or less effective, for achieving mediumship.

The acquisition of this type of mediumship exposes the aspirant to the danger of an induced state of mental passivity during which the mind may register vibrations broadcast from some terrestrial centre such as that provided by the recently constituted "Polaire Society" and recognized by the H. B. of L.

The cultivation of spiritism under all its different aspects either for amusement or pseudo-scientific investigation leads to serious consequences when occult adepts rely upon such manifestations for spiritual and material guidance. One is appalled at the thought that even the destinies of nations may become subject to occult direction emanating from

spiritistic séances. In connection herewith, the following clipping shows
the operation of these methods on persons prominent in political life. As
everyone knows, Mrs. Snowden, now Viscountess Snowden, is the wife
of the then (1930) Chancellor of the Exchequer, and a woman of great
personal influence.

MRS. SNOWDEN & THE SPIRITS
MESSAGE WHEN SHE CAME TO LONDON
SIR OLIVER LODGE IN DOWNING-STREET

Space "pulsating with life and mind" was a picture of the universe
drawn by Sir Oliver Lodge in a lecture which he delivered last
night at 11, Downing-street, Mr. Snowden's official residence as
Chancellor of the Exchequer.

Sir Oliver was speaking on the reality of the spiritual world,
his lecture being delivered in connection with the Industrial Law
Bureau of the Young Women's Christian Association. It was held
in two reception rooms on the first floor of No. 11. Sir Oliver
stood in the doorway between, so that he could be heard in either
room.

Mrs. Philip Snowden, who presided, recalled an experience of her
own when in 1906 she and Mr. Snowden first came to London.

"We got tired of hotel life," said Mrs. Snowden, "and obtained
rooms in Lambeth Palace-road. The following morning a letter
came to me at this address which nobody in the world could have
known. I opened this letter and it looked like nonsense.

"Scrutinising it carefully, I divided the letters and they made
sentences the substance of which was that, I must put myself into
friendly relationship with someone who had passed over—into
the ether—because that persons work would not be effective if I
did not do it, and my work here would not be so good as it might

be if I failed to do it. There was an accompanying note which said that this message was delivered to me at a spiritualist meeting, in Lancaster, and the writer sent the message on."
The Daily Telegraph, October 29th 1930.

The physical force of "Kundalini" expended by people in these "communications with the unseen drain their vital energy to such an extent that, when such practices are indulged in for an appreciable length of time, their nervous systems may be seriously impaired. A "Ouija" medium, after a week's consecutive sittings will feel a sense of heaviness and oppression about the solar plexus at certain hours. This sensation is shortly followed by serious physical weakness, manifest in sports and athletics. Presently, the medium—now a potential medical patient—will be unable to sleep at night.

Cracks, bangs, knocks, etc., will mark an approaching state of obsession. People whose psychic experiments have brought them to this degree of development, generally cut short further adventures in this field of science and theology. These have learned that there is indeed something beyond the obvious, and that after this stage of induced experimental mediumship has been achieved the way is open for such states of mind variously known to psychopathic doctors and priests as lunacy, possession, obsession, alternating personality and sadism.

Mediumship does not imply power. A medium is a receiver and, as such, furthers the will of another. The fakirs of India are mediums.

That these phenomena are real has been proved by such prominent scientists as Crooks, Richet and Flammarion and the mediumistic exploits of such persons as D. I. Home are so well known and attested that we will give but one short extract here from page 171 of *The Rosicrucian*, quoting a speech by Lord Lindsay, Senior Grand Warden of England, for the benefit of persons who may happen to have no acquaintance with the subject.

"I may mention that on another occasion I was sitting with Mr. Home and Lord Adare and a cousin of his. During the sitting Mr. Home went into a trance, and in that state was carried out of the window in the room next to where we were, and was brought in at our window. The distance between the windows was about seven feet six inches and there was not the slightest foothold between them, nor was there more than a twelve inch projection to each window, which served as a ledge to put flowers on."

What are we to think when we read in John Drinkwater's remarkable book on Charles James Fox that Sir Francis Dashwood was Chancellor of the Exchequer under George III?

Regarding the career of Sir Francis, we here read the following. The comment concerns John Wilkes whose "ambition to be admitted into the childish and blasphemous fraternity notorious as the Monks of Medmenham was frustrated by the claims of superior profligacy advanced by the fourth Lord Sandwich, with whom he competed for election. His resentment against that nobleman and Sir Francis Dashwood, the founder of the Society, was not appeased by the success of an exploit that diverted the town. Wilkes contrived to let a baboon loose upon one of the orgiastic rites at Medmenham that was being conducted in darkness, and had the satisfaction of throwing his victims into hysterics at the apparition of what their befuddled wits took to be the devil."[60]

What indeed can be deduced from such an historical fact as that Lord Sandwich, "notable even in that age as a corrupter of morals", was Secretary of State?

The obvious conclusion we can draw is that men either corrupt or easily bought are men easily blackmailed just as those who, being victims of their own greed, are amenable to bribery.

Spiritism is the fundamental mystery of most secret societies and the drug traffic is its chief commercial secret.

A clipping from the London *Daily Telegraph* of Nov. 29, 1930, which we reproduce, will give the reader an excellent idea of the problem of Modern Spiritism.

SPIRITUALISTS AND THE LAW
TEXT OF A BILL TO GRANT RELIEF

IMMUNITY FROM PROSECUTION
SOME FAMOUS CASES RECALLED

The text was issued yesterday of the Spiritualism and Psychical Research (Exemption) Bill, a measure promoted by Mr. Kelly, M. P. for Rochdale, and ten other members of the Socialist party.

It is designed to relieve spiritualists and mediums from prosecution under the enactments relating to witchcraft and vagrancy whilst they are "genuinely exercising their psychic powers, whether in religious practice or scientific investigation."

Although the bill appears to meditate only a change in the criminal law, it is obvious that if placed on the Statute Book it must to some extent affect the attitude towards spiritualism of judges who administer the common law and the principle of equity.

If, for example, spiritualism, séances, and mediums are to be recognised as no longer inimical to the public well-being, it difficult to see how the civil courts could hold, as they have done on several occasions, that a bequest of an institution for the training of mediums and the furtherance of spiritualism generally is void, as being against public policy. By his will Sir Arthur Conan Doyle left bequests to three spiritualistic institutions.

On this aspect of the matter it is interesting to recall how, heretofore, the cult of spiritualism has been received in the High Court. It has figured, though not as a vital issue, in actions for libel and slander. The typical cases of Archdeacon T. Colley v. J. N. Maskelyne, in 1907, and Radcliffe Hal l v. Lane Fox Pitt, in 1920, will be remembered.

MEDIUMS'COPYRIGHT

It has also been a more intimate issue in a copyright case, Cummins v. Bond, which came before Mr. Justice Eve three or four years ago. The question for solution in that case was whether the copyright in a communication said to have been made at a séance by the spirit of a Glastonbury monk was vested in the woman medium who received it, or in the enthusiastic sitter to whom she dictated it and who wished to publish it.

The sitter claimed that he owned the copyright, as the author was a spirit and had only used the medium as an instrument of transmission. On the other hand, the medium claimed the copyright on the ground that she was not a mere amanuensis, but was in communion with the spirit of the deceased monk, and was therefore joint author of the message.

With customary directness the judge disregarded the pretension of both parties that the communication had an ultra-terrestrial origin. He dealt with it as coming from a terrestrial author, and held the medium to be the author and therefore the holder of the copyright.

Long memories may also revive the case of Lyon and Home, one of the most notable cases ever brought into a Chanery Court.

A wealthy widow made a gift of £30,000 to Daniel Douglas Home, the last celebrated of the mediums of his time (the 'sixties), and gave him also a reversionary interest in another sum of similar amount. She did this believing that she was fulfilling the wish of her husband, whose spirit Home had invoked. Subsequently she rued her generosity, and brought an action to have the gifts set aside.

Vice-Chancellor Giffard heard the case, and for nine days the court listened to talk about table rapping, knotted handkerchiefs, and other phenomena. In setting aside the gifts Giffard characterised the manifestations which had influenced the lady as:

"Mischievous nonsense, well calculated on the one hand to delude the vain, the weak, the foolish, and the superstitious, and on the other hand to assist the projects of the needy and the adventurer."

LORD DARLING' S DICT A

There is no need to strain the memory severely for an instance of judicial criticism of the claims of spiritualists made by Mr. Justice Darling.

A theatrical agent sued theatrical producers for damages for alleged failure to carry out an agreement to ace the Criterion Theatre at his disposal for a public séance. Merely mentioning that the plaintiff won his case, and was awarded £200 damages, the comments of the judge may be quoted full, because reference was made the statute which it is now sought to fiend:

"It is an open question whether the manifestations given by mediums are genuine or mere tricks by which people are able to represent that there is communication with the next world. I should myself come to the conclusion that there is no certain desire to deceive or impose, but that it is desired that people should be puzzled as to whether there is a genuine manifestation of spirits or whether it is trickery.

"There are those who believe that the spirits can communicate in this world with those they have known, through some medium. Their time is so unoccupied in the next world, and it is such a dreary place, that the v are perfectly ready to come to the Criterion and attend matinees, and not to look on from the stage, but be on the stage.

"Before even they get on the stage they are counting the pennies in Mr.__'s overcoat or the buttons on it, and reading a jumble of German and English nonsense.

"On the other hand, there are those who are capable of supposing that this really is a kind of existence imposed for eternity upon those who have ceased to exist in life. If that is so, 'well may we weep for friends who die'.

"All they (the plaintiffs) desired to do was to give an exhibition which would leave some people in doubt as to whether it was real divination by means of the dead or some trickery. No magistrate ought to convict them on this account under the statute of George IV."

LICENSED CLAIRVOYANTS

In the bill now before Parliament it is proposed that spiritualists shall be given immunity from prosecution, provided that there is no intention to defraud. The following are specifically mentioned as coming within the scope of the bill:

Promoter, chairman, or other official, Lecturer or speaker, Clairvoyant, Medium.

For the purposes of the bill, "medium" and "clairvoyant" are defined as meaning a person "holding a certificate or licence of fitness to practise either as a medium or clairvoyant, or in both capacities, such certificate or licence to be issued by registered or properly constituted spiritualistic or psychical societies, or a joint committee representing such societies, or such other certifying or licensing body as may be approved by one of his Majesty's Principal Secretaries of State."

The Societies of Psychical Research, both in England and America, exist today as scientific centres for information and investigation of spirit phenomena. Persons interested in these "mysteries" would do well to avail themselves of their protection and the facilities they afford for serious work. The English Society was founded in 1882 by Henry Sidgwick, Edmund Gurney, Frederick Meyers, W. T. Barrett and others.

For root of this movement see Chapter XXII.

For development of this movement see Chapters CVIII, CIX, CX, CXV.

CHAPTER LXXXI

THE EASTERN STAR
(FOUNDED 1850)

THIS ORDER HAS five degrees and was founded for the wives and daughters of Masons in America by Robert Morris in 1850. It has also been worked in Scotland.

Jephthah's Daughter	Daughter's Degree
Ruth	Widow's Degree
Esther	Wife's Degree
Martha	Sister's Degree
Electa	Benevolent Degree

For root of this movement see Chapter XLVII.

CHAPTER LXXXII

THE IRISH REPUBLICAN BROTHERHOOD
(I. R. B.) THE FENIANS
(FOUNDED 1857–1858)

CONCERNING THIS FAMOUS Secret Society, Captain Pollard writes:

"From its earliest days to the present time the I. R. B. has existed as a militant revolutionary secret society, with the avowed object of separating Ireland from all connection with the British Empire and establishing an independent Republican Government.[61]

"The founders of this movement were Colonel John O'Mahoney and a barrister, Michael Doheney, both of whom had fled from Ireland for their share in the rising of 1848. Both these men took refuge in France, at that time a hot-bed of secret Carbonarist societies, such as the *Communistes Revolulionnaires, the Constitutional Society* with its 'Acting Company', the Seasons and many others, and it was in Paris that these two fugitives lived with James Stephens, the real head and organizer of the Fenian movement, who was also a refugee."

"In 1857 a messenger was sent from New York to James Stephens, then in Dublin, asking him to get up an organization in Ireland on resources provided from the States (U. S. A.); and it is clear that Stephens had already cut-and-dried plans in his mind as to how this was to be done. He stated his terms, which were agreed to, and on St. Patrick's Day 1858, the I. R. B. movement was initiated by Stephens and Luby in Dublin."

In 1859 the I. R. B. exacted the following oath; "I, A. B., in the presence of Almighty God, do solemnly swear allegiance to the Irish Republic now virtually established; and that I will do my utmost, at every risk, while life lasts, to defend its independence and integrity; and finally that I will yield implicit obedience in all things, not contrary to the laws of God, to the commands of my superior officers. So help me God. Amen."

"The organization made rapid headway, but the weight of the Roman Catholic Hierarchy was surging against the movement, and in due course the Brotherhood was excommunicated; in 1861 no Fenian could get absolution."

In reference to the founding of the Fenian society in America, Heckethorn fifty years ago had written the following:

"In Nov. 1863, the Fenian organization assumed a new character. A grand national convention of delegates met at Chicago and avowed the object of the Brotherhood, namely, the separation of Ireland from England, and the establishment of an Irish republic, the same changes being first to be effected in Canada. Another grand convention was held in 1864 at Cincinnati, the delegates at which represented some 250,000 members, each of which members was called upon for a contribution of five dollars, and this call, it is said, was promptly responded to…. About the same time a Fenian Sisterhood was established, and the ladies were not inactive; for in two months from their associating they returned upwards of £200,000 sterling to the Fenian Exchequer for the purpose of purchasing arms and other war material."[62]

To raise money the Fenians issued bonds redeemable 90 days after the establishment of the future Irish Republic.

Availing ourselves of the remarkable documentation furnished by Captain Pollard we gather the following facts:

"The American Fenian Brotherhood was a separate organization, distinct from the Irish Fenian Brotherhood or I. R. B. having its own leaders; but both organizations were on the same lines and had their officers, both civil and military oaths, emblems, and passwords, funds and stores of arms."[63]

All was well till Sept. 14, 1865 when "the Dublin authorities, who were thoroughly well informed, raided the offices of *The Irish People* and arrested the staff."

James Stephens was arrested with the rest but "escaped through the nominal complicity of a warder, John Breslin, who was also a member of the I. R. B." "Stephens had received some twenty-five thousand pounds, little of which was spent in Ireland, and in later years it was a matter of common knowledge that Stephens, besides being Head Centre, had also an agreement with the British Government, which threw a peculiar light on his immunity from arrest and his later escape from prison and leisurely retreat to France."[64]

On March 5, 1867, "Colonel" Kelly, heading a dissident group of Fenians, established a Directory separate from the original I. R. B. in London.

"Kelly, it should be noted, was the inventor of the *Committee of Safety*, later known as the *Assassination Committee*, whose function was to shoot people suspected of 'treason' to the Brotherhood."

"In 1869 new influences in America and Paris succeeded in reform-ing the I. R. B. Directorate in London, and the organization became not only a mainspring of revolutionary endeavour in Ireland, but a defi-nite element in the complex machinery of world-revolution." In March 1865, the Fenians joined the amalgamation of subversive Secret Societies under Karl Marx, known as the *International Association of Working Men*, founded in London on September 28th.

"It is, at all events, clear that Marx and the leaders of the I. R. B. were in close touch, and that Marx knew, even if the mass of Irish dupes did not, that the Irish revolutionary dream of the I. R. B. and Fenian leaders was no merely nationalist rebellion, but was to be a social revolution."[65]

"The function of the Fenian 'General' Cluseret and his relation to the International are not precisely clear, but he appears to have acted as a chief of the military rather than the civil side of the secret Lodges. During his stay in England on his Fenian mission he paid particular attention to the problem of how London might be captured, held and burnt…. After the suppression of the Paris branch of the *Internationale* it was Cluseret who organized the workers as a secret communist revolutionary society."

The more recent activities of the I. R. B. should be followed in connection with The Clan-na-Gael.

For root of this movement see Chapter LXXVII.

For development of this movement see Chapter LXXXVIII.

CHAPTER LXXXIII

PHOENIX SOCIETY OF SKIBBEREEN
(FOUNDED 1858)

IN OUR ENUMERATION of subversive societies we must include the Phoenix Society of Skibbereen of which Captain Pollard writes the following in *The Secret Societies of Ireland* (page 46).

"In 1858 a premature organization, contrived to revive the tenets of the Young Irishmen of ten years earlier, was founded at Skibbereen by Jeremiah O'Donovan Rossa and James Stephens. Both these men were later to attain notoriety in criminal annals, but the *Phoenix Society* was abortive. Attacked by the priests it was suppressed."

This society is interesting to us on account of the subsequent career of James Stephens, one of its founders, who had previously been identified with the Fenian movement.

For root of this movement see Chapter LXXXII.

CHAPTER LXXXIV

L'ALLIANCE ISRAELITE UNIVERSELLE
(A BRANCH OF JEWISH MASONRY)
(FOUNDED 1860)

IF, AS IT has been appropriately defined, Judaism is a sect, the creation of the Alliance Israélite Universelle which took place in 1860 can be regarded as that of its exoteric centre.

It was founded in 1860 by Aristide Astruc, Isidor Cahen, Jules Carvalho, Narcisse Leven, Eugene Manuel and Charles Netter. Its first president was Konigswarter. Adolphe Cremieux was president from 1863–1867 and again from 1868–1880.

In 1840, the world had been startled by the news of the fearful murder of Père Thomas at Damascus. Serious investigations had resulted in the conviction of three Jews who had confessed to the commission of the abominable crime for Jewish ritual purposes of procuring human blood.

The indignation of the whole world rising against Jewry made its prominent members realize the danger threatening their newly acquired emancipation in most countries, and they made a concerted effort to disprove Jewish guilt in the Damascus affair. Foremost among them had been Moses Monte fiore, Adolphe Cremieux and Solomon Munk. Yet, the real inspirer of the Alliance Israelite Universelle was Hirsch Kalisher, Rabbi of Thorn (Russia) and its enthusiastic exponent, Moses Hess.

The chief aim of the Alliance Israelite Universelle was political, and was clearly expressed in the report circulated after its foundation in which was stated: *All important faiths are represented in the world by nations, that is to say, they are incarnated in governments especially interested in them and officially authorized to represent them and speak for them only. Our faith alone is without this important advantage; it is represented neither by a state nor by a society, nor does it occupy a clearly defined territory.*

The Alliance Israelite Universelle therefore was destined to be the governmental representative of all Jews from whatever country they lived in under the authority of their secret Kahal or community rule.

The first political manifestation of the Alliance Israelite Universelle took place at the Berlin Congress in 1878 where it was represented by three of its delegates: Kann, Netter and Veneziani.

The link between the Alliance Israelite Universelle and Freemasonry was for many years Adolphe Crémieux and Masonic writers have asserted that the 18th degree, conferred by the Grand Orient, makes the initiate, if not a member, at any rate a supporter of the Alliance.

The Alliance Israelite Universelle saw its dream of international Jewish Government shattered when Zionism emerged and came to the fore in 1897. It is noteworthy that the "Prophet" of Zionism: Ahad Ha'am (Asher Ginsberg) was a member of the Alliance Israelite Universelle and a disciple of Charles Netter. The avowed aims of the A. I. U., namely a super-government of the world and a universal religion, both to be Judaic, are being steadily pursued by the "Jewish World Agency" functioning today.

CHAPTER LXXXV

THE INTERNATIONAL
(FIRST AND SECOND)
(FOUNDED 1860)

IN HIS EARLY days, Karl Marx, later to be the moving spirit of the First International, edited a paper in Paris, *Annales Franco-Allemandes*, the organ of a secret society. This paper had been founded by Arnold Riige, a disciple of Mazzini. Marx met Riige through Henri Heine, the celebrated poet.[66]

Heckethorn, in his *Secret Societies of All Ages and Countries* gives an interesting synopsis of the early phases of this movement destined ultimately to form the keystone of subversion throughout the world.[67]

"The first attempt at an international society was made by a small number of German workmen in London, who had been expelled from France in 1839 for taking part in the riots in Paris. Its members consisted of Germans, Hungarians, Poles, Danes and Swedes. Of the few English members Ernest Jones was one. The society was on friendly terms with the English Socialists, the Chartists, and the London French Democratic Society. Out of that friendship sprang the Society of the Fraternal Democrats, who were in correspondence with a number of democratic societies in Belgium. In November, 1847, a German Communist Conference was held in London, at which Dr. Karl Marx (real name Mordechai) was present. In the manifesto then put forth it was declared that the aim of the Communists was the overthrow of the rule of the capitalists by the acquisition of political power. The practical measures by which this was to be effected were the abolition of private property in land; the centralization of credit in the hands of the State—the leading agitators of course to be the chiefs of the State—by means of a national bank; the centralization of the means of transport in the hands of the State; national workshops; the reclamation and improvement of land; and the gratuitous education of all the children.

"In 1860, a Trade Unionist, Manhood Suffrage, and Vote by Ballot Association was established, of which G. Odger, a shoemaker, was chairman. As if it had not enough of what might be called legitimate work to do, the association also undertook to agitate in favour of Poland, for which purpose it co-operated with the National League for the Independence of Poland. The London International Exhibition of 1862 induced the French government to assist many French workmen with means to visit that exhibition... "and"... on the 5th August, all the delegates met at a dinner given to the m by their English colleagues at Freemason's Hall, where an address was read which formed, as it were, the foundation-stone of the International. The Imperial Commission that had enabled the French workmen to visit the London Exhibition had no doubt furnished them with return tickets. But several of the artisans made no use of their second halves, since profitable employment in London was found for them by their English brethren, so that they might form connecting links between the workmen of the two countries."

The next year, another meeting was arranged and this was followed by others. At last one was held in London on Sept. 24, 1864, presided over by Professor Beesly, at which it was finally determined to establish a permanent organization of the working people of the civilized world. The International Working Men's Association was thus founded. In *The Jewish Encyclopaedia*, Article on Karl Marx, we read that Mazzini and Marx were entrusted with the task of preparing the address and the constitution. Then came the big public meeting held on September 28, 1864 at St. Martin's Hall, which "declared the International Working Men's Association to be established and congresses were appointed to be held at different times and places to decide on the measures to be taken to found the working men's Eldorado. Many societies at first were affiliated, but dissensions soon broke out among them, and many, such as the Italian Working Men's Society, withdrew again."[68]

This withdrawal of the Italian section was doubtless influenced by its recognition of the subversion of the original scheme for the amelioration of industrial conditions by the Mazzinian revolutionary agents.

"At a meeting held in London, in 1865, the 're-establishment of Poland entire and independent' was again one of the questions discussed. The Paris delegates were for avoiding political questions; but Mr. Odger reminded them that Poland had furnished the occasion for the establishment of the association, and that the Conference must stand by the Polish cause."

In 1866, a meeting or congress was held at Geneva, where the abolition of standing armies, the destruction of the monopolies of great companies, and the transfer of railways and other means of locomotion to the people, were decided on. Another resolution favouring Polish Independence was passed and the report of Marx made in 1864 was adopted.

To anyone unversed in the intricacies of International Politics at that date, the introduction and predominance of the measures concerning Poland seem senseless. All the International societies which, at that time, were affiliated to that of Young Italy of which Mazzini, if not in every case the nominal founder, was in all cases the moving spirit, were controlled by a central committee of which the famous Italian Revolutionary was the presiding genius. In this committee centered also the political power of Carbonarism plus that of Masonry as well as that of Judaism which, functioning through Mazzini, Levi and Lemmi, found, in the dawning International, an easy means of fostering revolutions on foreign territory and a centre of agitation towards extorting the extension of rights and privileges to their "Jewish brothers" in Poland, which, at that date had the largest Jewish population of any country in the world. Thus, the International, later to become its most powerful agent and the tyrant of a nation, began to serve the Jewish International power.

We now obtain the further information to the effect that at the Congress of Bâle, held in 1869, Bakounine and Armand Levi fought for the control of the organization. "Bakounine, the Russian Nihilist, spoke thus without reserve: 'By social liquidation I mean expropriation of all existing proprietors, by the abolition of the political and legal state, which is the sanction and only guarantee of all property as now existing, and of all that is called legal right; and the expropriation, in fact, everywhere, and as much and as quickly as possible by the force of events and circumstances'."[69]

After such remarks, the International was evidently considered by its masters to have shown its mettle and to be deserving of better quarters. "A temple worthy of their cult was sought and found... near Geneva, where... a fine building, the Masonic Temple—*Temple Unique*... was procured. ... They put the name of Temple on their cards and bills. Their cult had gained a worthy shrine..."[70]

The further aims of the movement are thus described by Heckethorn:

"...At the time when the International was founded, the French Empire was as yet in all its strength and.... its ministers looked upon themselves as small Machiavellis when they permitted the International (which claimed to be a social, non-political organization), to grow in order, some day, to use it against a mutinous bourgeoisie. The Emperor had an opportunity on September 2, at Sedan, and the Empress on September 4, at Paris, to judge of the value of such policy. However, the scheme of the association having been settled in London in 1864, the organizers opened at Paris a *bureau de correspondence*, which was neither formally interdicted nor regularly authorized by the Prefect and the Minister. But the constantly growing power of the International shown by the strikes of Roubaix, Amiens, Paris, Geneva, etc. after a time compelled the government either to direct or to destroy it. The Parisian manifesto read at Geneva was stopped at the French frontier; but M. Rouher agreed to admit it into France, if the association would insert some passages thanking the Emperor for what he had done for the working classes—a suggestion which was received with derision by the members. In the meantime the old revolutionary party, of which Mazzini, Garibaldi, Blanqui, and Ledru-Rollin were the oracles, looked with suspicion on the foundation of the International; for, as this last declared that it would not meddle with politics, the others called out, Treason! And thus the two parties were soon in a condition of violent opposition. In 1867, the Congress of Lausanne voted against war, but at the same moment the other fraction of the demagogues, assembled at Geneva, under pretense of forming a congress of peace, declared war on all tyrants and oppressors of the people. However, the two parties, the bourgeois demagogues and the workmen demagogues, eventually united; and thus it came to pass that by virtue of this pact the International took part in two revolutionary manifestations which occurred about six weeks after—the one at the tomb of Manin in the cemetery of Montmartre, and the other on the following day on the Boulevard Montmartre, to protest against the French occupation of Rome. The International having thus been carried away to declare war against the government, the latter determined to prosecute it. The association was declared to be dissolved, and fifteen of the leaders were each fined a hundred francs. The International taking no notice of the decree of dissolution, a second prosecution was instituted, and nine of the accused were condemned to imprisonment for three months. The International now hid itself amidst the multitude of working men's societies of all descriptions that were either authorized or at least tolerated, and made enormous progress so that its chiefs at last declared themselves able to do without any extraneous support. 'The International', said one of the speakers at the Bâle Congress (1869), 'is and must be a state within states; let these go on as suits them, until our state is the strongest. Then, on the ruins of these, we shall erect our own fully prepared, such as it exists in every section.'

"On September 3rd 1870, the disaster of Sedan became known at Paris. On the next day, Lyons, Marseilles, Toulouse, and Paris proclaimed the Republic. This simultaneous movement was the result of an understanding existing between the leading members of the International in the various parts of France; but that the 'Jules Favres and Gambettas,' that *vermine bourgeoise*, as the International called them, should obtain any share of power, was very galling to the demagogues. At Lyons and Marseilles, however, the supreme power fell into the hands of the lowest wretches. The Commune installed at Lyons began its work by raising the red flag—that of the International. At Paris the association pretended at first to be most anxious to fight the Prussians. When the battalions were sent to the front, however, it was found that those comprising most International were the most ready 'to fall back in good order,' or even to fly in great disorder at the first alarm; and General Clement Thomas pointed out this instructive fact to the readers of the *Journal Officiel*. But when a few Prussian regiments entered Paris, the International , through its central committee, announced that the moment for action was come; and so the members seized the cannons scattered in various parts of the city, and then began that series of excesses, for which the Commune will always enjoy an infamous notoriety. Its first sanguinary act was the assassination of Generals Lecomte and Clement Thomas.[71]

"One would have supposed that the International would disavow the Communists: but, on the contrary, it approved of their proceedings. Flames were still ascending from the Hotel de Ville when already numerous sections of the International throughout Europe expressed their admiration of the conduct of the Parisian outcasts.

"At Zurich, at a meeting of the members of the International, it was declared that 'the struggle maintained by the Commune of Paris was just and worthy, and that all thinking men ought to join in the contest'."

Thus they agreed with Armand Levi and Jewish Masonry!

In 1872, another Jew, Karl Marx, transferred "the seat of the General Council to New York, in care of his faithful follower F. A. Sorge", his co-religionist.[72]

There the organization degenerated into a gang of Anarchist-revolutionaries. In 1876 it was dissolved.

Numerous efforts to re-create the First International were made by Marx assisted by Jules Guesde and in 1889 they founded the Second International, the development of which was retarded by internal dissensions. In 1905 however a programme of unification, elaborated at Amsterdam, was accepted by the contending factions.[73]

For root of this movement see Chapter LIII.

For development of this movement see Chapter CXXV.

CHAPTER LXXXVI

THE KU-KLUX KLAN
(FOUNDED 1865)

THE KU-KLUX KLAN was the name of an American secret association formed by the Whites of the Southern States for self-protection after the Civil war.

It was started at 1865 at Pulaski, Tennessee, as a club for young men. The period of organization of the K. K. K. lasted from 1865 to 1868. It absorbed other societies of similar aims such as the Knights of the White Camelia, the White Brotherhood, the White League, the Pale Faces, Black Cavalry, White Rose, etc.

Apart from the protection of whites, one of its chief aims was opposition to a government based on negro suffrage such as the North wanted to impose on the South.

The Klan denominated the entire South as the Invisible Empire under the rule of a Grand Wizard: General N. B. Forrest. Each state was a Realm under a Grand Dragon; each county a Province under a Grand Giant, etc.

The avowed principles were the maintenance of peace and order, of the laws of God, of the political and social supremacy of the white race and also the prevention of the intermingling of the races.

It showed strenuous opposition to the "scallawags" and "carpet-baggers" as they called the Northern Whites who incited the negroes to commit all kinds of depredations against the Whites of the South.

In 1871 and 1872, the United States Congress enacted a series of "Force Laws" to break the K. K. K. By that time however the negro was once more subdued and the K. K. K.'s central organization was disbanded.

Its spirit however survived and reasserted itself in 1915 when it was revived.

For development of this organization see Chapter CXXIII.

CHAPTER LXXXVII

SOCIETAS ROSICRUCIANA IN ANGLIA
(FOUNDED 1866)

FOR AN HISTORICAL sketch of the Societas Rosicruciana in Anglia, the cover name for modern Illuminism, we can do no better than turn to such an authority as its historian William Wynn Westcott, erstwhile Supreme Magus of the Society.

The following items of information are gleaned from his *History of the Societas Rosicruciana in Anglia*, published in 1910.[74] The official statement of the aims of the Society reads as follows :—"The aim of the Society is to afford mutual aid and encouragement in working out the great problems of Life and in searching out the secrets of Nature; to facilitate the study of the system of philosophy founded upon the Cabala and the doctrines of Hermes Trismegistus, which was inculcated by the original Fratres Rosae-Crucis of Germany, A. D. 1450; and to investigate the meaning and symbolism of all that now remains of the wisdom, art and literature of the ancient world."

"The Societas Rosicruciana in Anglia was founded in 1866 by Frater Robert Wentworth Little, an eminent Freemason with much literary talent, and of great personal popularity. He was Secretary of the Province of Middlesex, and Secretary of the Royal Masonic Institution for Girls. He became the first Supreme Magus and Master General of the College in 1867. His knowledge and authority emanated from two sources, and

were supplemented by the learning and researches of several other prominent students of occult philosophy. Brother William Henry White, the
Grand Secretary of England, preserved certain Rosicrucian papers[75] which
had come into his possession on attaining office in 1810, at Freemason's
Hall, and of these he made no use; Brother Little found these papers and
used them. At the same time, and with the object of re-constituting a
Rosicrucian College in London, he availed himself of certain knowledge
and authority which belonged to Brother Kenneth R. H. Mackenzie, who
had, during a stay in Germany in earlier life, been in communication
with German Adepts who claimed a descent from previous generations of
Rosicrucians. German Adepts had admitted him to some grades of their
system, and had permitted him to attempt the formation of a group of
Masonic students in England, who under the Rosicrucian name might
form a partly esoteric society. With this license and with the manuscripts
of ritual information, which Brother White had discovered in the vaults of
Freemason's Hall, Fratres R. W. Hughan, Woodman, O'Neal Haye, Irwin
and some others, the present English rituals were adopted, and have been
in use with some modifications made by Dr. Woodman and his successor,
ever since the first regular meeting of the Society.

"The basic rule of the new Society stated that only Master Masons of
good standing and repute should be admitted to membership, thus drawing a new distinction, of which we have no previous record; for earlier
English Rosicrucian Colleges had no Masonic basis, and some fraternities
abroad certainly admitted women on equal terms, of which fact there is
extant literary proof.

"See the curious document called 'The admission of Sigismund Bac-
strom, dated September 12th 1794'. This will be found reprinted in *The
Rosicrucian* of October, 1876. The only literary extant evidence of the
source of our Rosicrucian ritual from Brother W. H. White is contained
in a letter in possession of the Society. The share of Kenneth Mackenzie in
the origin of the Society depends at the present time on his letters to Dr.
Woodman and Dr. Westcott, and on his personal conversations during
the years 1876–1886 with Dr. Westcott.

"Fratres Hughan, Irwin, Hockley, Woodforde and Benjamin Cox have also contributed their personal knowledge on the subject.

"The original MSS. which Little possessed never came into the possession of the S. M., the late Dr. Woodman, and so were never received by the present Magus who has thus few proofs in writing of the historic basis, which he lays down in this sketch of the Society. The most natural conclusion is that Little returned these papers to some obscure portion of the records at Freemason's Hall, and that they are there still, although the present officials have not traced them. This explanation is very probable, because in September 1871, a Brother Mathew Cooke raised a complaint in Grand Lodge against Masonic officials for discovering, using and removing old manuscripts from the record rooms of Freemason's Hall. These papers supplied the basis for the reconstitution of the Order of the Red Cross of Constantine, as well as of the Rosicrucian Society. They were both Christian bodies, and their records had been hidden away since the time of the Grand Mastership of the Duke of Sussex, in 1813, who, favouring the Unitarian doctrine, did all in his power to remove Christian grades from notice.

"Our records include a letter from the Rev. T. F. Ravenshaw, Grand Chaplain of England, one of the earliest fratres of the Society, confirming much of the historic information which the author received from Dr. Woodman, Woodforde, Mackenzie and Irwin. This letter recites as follows:—(I) that the first S. M. Frater R. M. Little explained to him that the German Fraternity had an established regulation which permitted distinguished members to confer Rosicrucian grades in due order on suitable persons. (II) That a certain Venetian Ambassador to England in the last century had conferred Rosicrucian grades and knowledge on Students in England; these in their turn had handed on the rule and tradition to others, of whom one of the last survivors was Frater William Henry White, Grand Secretary of English Freemasonry from 1810 to 1857; he retired and lived until 1866. (III) From the papers he possessed Frater White admitted Frater Robert Wentworth Little. (IV) These papers came into Little's possession at Freemason's Hall on Frater White's retirement from office. (V) The rituals are mentioned as being imperfect for ceremonial open use."

The above contains much useful information for any reader who might later undertake research work not only on the Societas Rosicruciana in Anglia but also in its offshoots: Golden Dawn, Stella Matutina and Ordo Templi Orientis, etc. As to the organization of the Society, in order to enable the reader to understand the system on which it functions, we reprint herewith from *The Rosicrucian*, the Quarterly Record of the Society's transactions,[76] edited by Frater Robert Wentworth Little (S. M.) Master General and Frater William Robert Woodman, M. D., Secretary General, some of the articles governing its organization.

I.—That the meetings of the Society shall be held in London at such house as the majority of the members shall select, on the 2nd Thursdays in January, April, July and October in each year, at such time and place as the majority shall select.

II.—The first meeting in the year shall be considered as the obligatory meeting and any member unable to attend on that occasion or at the banquet meeting shall be required to send a written excuse to the Secretary-General. Each brother present at the banquet shall pay his quota towards the expenses thereof.

III.—The Master-general and the Officers shall be elected annually at the obligatory meeting and shall be induced into their several offices on the same evening. The Master-general shall then appoint the Assistant officers for the year.

IV.—No brother shall be eligible for election to the office of Master-general or Deputy Master-general unless he shall have served one year as an Ancient, and have attained the third Order; and no brother shall be eligible for the offices of Treasurer-general, Secretary-general, or Ancient, unless he be a member of the second Order.

V.—The Society shall, in conformity with ancient usage, be composed of nine classes or grades, and the number of brethren in each class shall be restricted as follows:—

| 1—or grade | Zelator | 33 |
| 2—or grade | Theoricus | 27 |

3—or grade	Practicus	21
4—or grade	Philosophus	18
	TOTAL	99

The above shall form the First Order

5—or grade of Adeptus Junior	15
6—or grade of Adeptus Major	12
7—or grade of Adeptus Exemptus	9
TOTAL	36

These brethren shall form the Second Order

8—or grade of Magister Templi	6
9—or Magus	3
TOTAL	9

These shall be considered as the Third (or highest) Order, and shall be entitled to seats in the Council of the Society. The senior member of the 9th grade shall be designated "Supreme Magus" and the two other members Senior and Junior Substitutes respectively. The grand total of membership shall thus be limited to 144, or the square of 12. The number of registered Novices or Aspirants shall not be restricted, but members only shall be permitted to be present at the ceremonial meetings of the Society.

VI.—The distinction of Honorary Member may be conferred upon eminent brethren, provided that their election to such membership shall be unanimous and that their number be strictly limited to 16, or the square of 4. An Honorary President, who must be a nobleman, and three Vice-Presidents, shall be selected from the honorary members. A Grand-Patron may also be elected in like manner.

VII.—No aspirant shall be admitted into the Society unless he be a Master Mason, and of good moral character, truthful, faithful and intelligent…

VIII.—Every Novice on admission to the grade of Zelator shall adopt a Latin motto, to be appended to his signature in all communications relating to the Society. This motto cannot under any pretense be afterwards changed, and no two brethren shall be at liberty to adopt the same motto….

The other articles, 20 in all, can be read in *The Rosicrucian*.

In 1877, the order of membership was rearranged to provide that in future, every College under the jurisdiction of England would be restricted to 36 subscribing members exclusive of members of the 9th grade: the only exception being the Metropolitan College which was to be permitted to enroll 72 members.

In *The Rosicrucian* the Society defines its aims in the following terms:—

"The object of the society being purely literary and antiquarian it is almost unnecessary to state that no interference with, or opposition to, any rite of Freemasonry is intended, or even tolerated: and it matters not to the members whether the aspirant be a disciple of pure and ancient Masonry, as interpreted by the Grand Lodge of England, or be enthusiastic follower of those rites which embrace the Haut s Grades, provided he be of good standing and possess sufficient ability to take part in the peculiar objects of research to which the society restricts itself—mystic and Rosicrucian lore.

"Thus the roll of the society displays names side by side, on the one hand ardent supporters of the high grades, and on the other their bitter opponents."

Those who have occupied the position of Supreme Magus in the order of their succession were:—

- R. Wentworth Little   1865–1878
- Dr. Robert Woodman   1878–1891
- Dr. William Wynn Westcott   1891–1925

Towards the close of the XIX Century, the membership of Rosicruciana in Anglia included the following personages:—

- Samuel Liddell MacGregor Mathers (Junior Sub Magus)
- Thomas Bowman Whytehead IX
- John Yarker IX
- George Kenning
- E. Waite

- Eliphas Levi
- Kenneth R. H. Mackenzie IX
- Major Irwin IX
- William James Hughan IX
    etc. etc.

The Annual Convocations were held in the Rosicrucian Temple at the Frascati restaurant, Oxford Street, London, W.

The foreign branches of this order were founded in—

Canada—in 1877 by M. W. Frater Col. W. B. Macleod Moore with Fratres Thomas Douglas Harrington as S. S. M. and George Longley as J. S. M. Four meetings a year at Masonic Hall, Maitland, Ontario.

The United States of America—in 1880 by M. W. Frater Charles E. Mayer IX, Supreme Magus of United States.

Germany—in 1902 by Theodore Reuss VIII (Initiated in the Pilgrim's Lodge 238, London).

Scotland—in 1877.

In connection with the statement made at the opening of this chapter that The Societas Rosicruciana in Anglia was modern Illuminism, the reader's attention must be drawn to the similarity of the grades of the modern Rosicrucian Society with those of Weishaupt's Bavarian Uluminism.

Much has been said and written by various and numerous English authorities on the subject of English Grand Lodge being in no wise connected with any outside societies, whether exoteric or esoteric or with foreign or, as they call it, "Continental" masonry.

We however submit the following suggestions as a logical deduction from a close study of the organization, activities and connections of the Societas Rosicruciana in Anglia.

English Grand. Lodge is today what it was intended to be at the time of its creation, by disciples of avowed Rosicrucianism, namely a dragnet or nursery. Under the guise of philanthropy, humanitarianism, democratic ideals, and the promise of material advancement, it attracts untold numbers of unsuspecting men. The sifting takes place from the time of their initiation. For those who are deemed useless to the further secret aims of

Masonry and therefore unworthy of climbing from the Master's chair in Grand Lodge to The Royal Arch degree, English Masonry will always remain what it was represented to be when they became candidates for initiation. They will be useful carriers of the legend that English Masonry believes in God and philanthropy. But, like Charity, English Grand Lodge covers a multitude of sins.... Above all, it covers Gnosticism under all its aspects; it is in fact its screen.

It is a common error to believe that the English Grand Lodge is an independent body which was formed in 1717. Logical deduction will show that, owing to its formation being the result of Rosicrucian effort, it always has been, and still must be, subject to the direction of its esoteric parent body, i. e. ROSICRUCIANISM or Manichean and Socinian Gnosticism.

Childish as may be the claim of English Grand Lodge as to its autonomy and independence, yet it has been most successfully defended by scores of English writers who attacked Masonic Societies and their subversive activities against state and religion. According to them English Grand Lodge was always exempted from such groups.

It is time to put an end to this legend. English Grand Lodge, the body which claims to represent English Freemasonry, is as much the child of Rosicrucianism today as it was in 1717 and has no more power or wish today to rebel against, or deny its parent, than it had then. As to Esoteric Rosicrucianism, this Esoteric body, mainly Cabalistic in its direction, always has been and is in truth international. It has penetrated every association, society or organization just as did the Illuminati of Bavaria at the Wilhelmsbad convent of 1782.

In the particular Gnostic Rosicruciana in Anglia, briefly sketched here, we see *internationalism* clearly depicted. At one time it was personified in Kenneth Mackenzie who, initiated and illuminized by the German Rosicrucian adepts, was later the connecting link between German, English and French Gnosticism, the latter represented at the time by Eliphas Levi (A. L. Constant).

Nearer to our own time, William Wynn Westcott is the connecting link of this international Rosicrucian-gnosticism. Prominent Grand

Lodge and Royal Arch Mason, he was also Supreme Magus of Rosicruciana in Anglia and Knight Kadosch etc.

His connections with John Yarker, as also with the French hermetist Papus and with the theosophist Blavatsky, were of an esoteric kind, but most important of all were his close relations with his brother Rosicrucian MacGregor Mathers and the German Theodore Reuss. For it is, we know, William Wynn Westcott, the respected English Grand Lodge and Royal Arch Mason, Supreme Magus of Rosicruciana in Anglia who, together with the Cabalist MacGregor Mathers, created the Rosicrucian branch known as the Order of the Golden Dawn. With Theodore Reuss he was closely associated with the foundation of the Ordo Templi Orientis which from Reuss and Karl Kellner's manuscripts is known to be phallic.

How far the reciprocal conferring of degrees in their respective orders between John Yarker, W. W. Westcott, Theodore Reuss, Engel and Papus is a case of interpenetration remains to be determined. John Yarker was the head of the Ancient and Primitive Rite of the Rite of Swedenborg, etc., Wm. Wynn Westcott, the Supreme Magus of Rosicruciana in Anglia, Theodore Reuss and Engel, heads of the German Illuminati and Ordo Templi Orientis, and Papus, head of the Martinists. We are fully aware of the Gnostic practices of these different rites but the student bent on a certain type of research will find interesting and instructive the study of the political activities of the different bodies mentioned. The author of *Light Bearers of Darkness*[77] has attempted to show part of the nefarious political game played by adepts of the Stella Matutina and Golden Dawn Orders, two of the occult branches of Rosicruciana in Anglia.

We reprint below two letters exchanged between William Wynn Westcott and the German Theodore Reuss which show the interlocking and international gnostic direction of those two late honoured members of English Grand Lodge Freemasonry.

It remains for the student to follow every line of enquiry to the point of concentration where all threads are gathered and systematically manipulated for the eventual destruction of Christian civilization.

It may lead to the B'nai B'rith, the Universal Israelite Alliance, India or Thibet, but in any case, a thorough and complete study of Rosicrucianism embracing a minute one of Rosicruciana in Anglia and its various branches will be a great step taken in the direction of uncovering much of the political and moral chaos of present day history of humanity.

Feb 14, 1902
Dear Bro. Reuss;

I have to acknowledge receipt of Illuminati papers and safely received and they shall be translated and considered and I will report upon what I can do—Best thanks.

As to the Swed. Riie the Lodge Holy Grail No. 15 is all right and Bro. Yarker is entirely within his right to give you, a known Master Mason of England, a Warrant for a Lodge, but he hesitates to issue written authority for 6 Lodges which your Latomia[78] says are not regular. I *had* got his permission to make a Prov. Gd. Lodge of Germania for you but now he hesitates, because he does not want to have half the German Masonic World condemning him—as well as half the English, who condemn him for the A. & P. Rite.

Please write to him John Yarker, Esq. West Didsbury, near Manchester Eng. and get his authority to go on, at present my hands are tied.

With best wishes,
Believe me,
Yours sincerely,
W. W. Westcott.
To Theodor Reuss
Societas Rosicruciana in Anglia
Dr. Wm. Wynn Westcott S. M. J. X.
Memorandum from the High Council 396, Camden Road, N.

Aug 26, 1902
Care Frater,

I have duly recd. your card & letter & Report, for all which best thanks. I hope you are well again. I am sorry you missed seeing my Bro. Gardner. I note what you say about the Illuminati and hereby accept the position of Regent, and must find a good man to work it up. Do I understand that Engel is now out of the order? I have not heard any more from him.

Re Rosics.

Your fratres must each choose a Latin motto; mine is "Quod scis, nescis."—even what you know—you don't really know—is a free translation—I will read your Report on Second Thursday in October to the High Council and Met. Coll.

There must be a lot of Rosic M. S. S. lying hid in your country, make every effort to find some. We have copies of two here. I will ask the H. C. about the use of Library. I propose to keep German contributions for buying further Books for it, and for that alone. You might look out to buy any German Rosic books for us.

Yours sincerely,
Wynn Westcott.

For root of this movement see Chapter XXII.
For development of this movement see Chapters CIX, CX, CXV.

CHAPTER LXXXVIII

THE CLAN-NA-GAEL (V. C.)
(FOUNDED 1869)

IN HIS OFT quoted book, *The Secret Societies of Ireland*, Captain H. B. C. Pollard, late of the Staff of the Chief of Police, Ireland, gives much valuable information concerning the Clan-na-Gael (See page 69 et seq.).

"In 1869 a new secret Irish-American organization was formed, known as the Clan-na-Gael. It traces its origin back through a permanent secret society known as the Knights of the Inner Circle, which, in turn, descended from the Knights of St. Patrick, known as the Ancient Order of Hibernians today. It was originally a seceding circle (The Brian Boru) of the United Irishmen, an American society tracing back to 1789." By 1873, the Clan had absorbed all independent Irish secret societies save that of "The Irish Confederation" of Jeremiah O'Donovan Rossa with which it had reached an arrangement for mutual toleration. "The original organizer of the Clan had called it the United Brotherhood, and in all its work a simple letter cipher composed of the next letter in the alphabet after the one really meant, was utilised. The secret name of the Clan being the United Brotherhood, it was therefore designated and spoken of as the V. C. Ireland was known as 'Jsfmboe', and so on. To this day the Clan speaks and writes of the I. R. B. as the S. C. "Up to 1881 the Clan-na-Gael was governed by an executive body, the F. C, and had an annually elected chairman. A Revolutionary Directory, the 'R. D.' consisted of seven members[79] ... Great secrecy shrouded the R. D. and the names of members were only known to the delegates and three 'senior Guardians' of each 'Camp' of the Clan.

"These Lodges or 'Camps' were known in cipher as 'D's'; each had a number and an outward innocent name, such as the Emmett Literary Association. The essential precaution for the maintenance of secrecy was the rule that all documents, when read, had to be burnt before the Brotherhood, a rule also common to the I. R. B. of today."

"An open Irish movement had been evolving in the States[80] and a great Irish Convention was held at Chicago in November, 1881, where all kinds of Irish associations were to be represented by delegates who would be addressed on the subject of the Land League. By a clever political manoeuvre the Clan secured the office of Chairman to one of its members, the Rev. George Betts, and as he had the right of appointment of all members of committees, they were enabled to nominate a Clan-na-Gael majority and force the Clan views on the whole body of the Convention.

"In 1882 the Clan, which had for long controlled the secret organization in America, now also controlled all the various open Irish societies and associations which had been represented at the Convention. The mechanism of control was simple—the whole influence of the Clan was exerted to secure to their members a preponderant representation as office-holders in these associations, and it soon became recognised that membership of the Clan was an indispensable preliminary to advancement in local Irish affairs.[81]

"The American Clan-na-Gael had concentrated all Irish organizations, however innocuous, in the body of the National League,[82] and had, by controlling the Committee of the League by its own members, thereby possessed itself not only of a vast field from which to draw funds and recruits, but of the whole coordinated political power of the Irish organizations in America. The process developed by the I. R. B. in Ireland was analogous; through its members they were represented on the Committees and Councils of practically every organization which, in the opinion of its leaders, could be of use to it. The identity of the I. R. B. men was always a secret.

"The secret power of the Brotherhood was brought to bear on all questions of appointment to positions and offices in various open associations, and it was its influence and corruption which achieved those mysterious appointments to position of persons singularly devoid of merit, which were, and are, a marked feature of Irish life...

"In so far as the activist military policy of the I. R. B. was concerned, the period from 1895 to 1912 was practically negative.

"The I. R. B. had always held that membership of any sectarian secret society, such as the A. 0. H., or the Orange Society was incompatible with membership of the I. R. B.[83]

"However, the A. O. H. in America has for many years been under the direct control of the Clan-na-Gael which also influences through the A. O. H. such American Catholic Associations as are not distinctly Irish, such as the Knights of Columbus, a Catholic Fraternal Society."

In the year 1912 "the action of the North in arming had its immediate repercussion in the South... On November 25th 1913 *The Irish Volunteers*, as distinct from the Ulster Volunteers, had been formally instituted."

"The outbreak of war introduced a new element in the shape of an alliance between the I. R. B., the Clan-na-Gael, and Germany."

Casement, whose political activities were ruled by the two Germans, Albert Ballin of the Hamburg-American line and Professor Kuno Meyer, "had been active in the councils of the Irish Volunteers and at the date of the outbreak of war was in the United States on business connected with the relationship between the I. R. B. and the Clan-na-Gael... On the 3rd Nov. 1914, he reached Berlin and laid before the German Foreign Office the suggestion of alliance between the Irish Republicans and Germany, and established a line of communication via the American Clan-na-Gael with revolutionary Ireland. From Berlin, he communicated with Judge Cohalan and John Devoy, the Clan Leaders in the States, who, in turn, maintained communication with the I. R. B. in Ireland through emissaries and an established letter-carrying service on craft crossing between Ireland and America.[84]

"The arrangements between the Clan-na-Gael as representing the I. R. B. and the German Government are amply set forth in such documents as the British Government has yet disclosed. e. g. in the White Paper, *Documents relative to the Sinn Fein movement*, published by H. M. Stationery office in 1921."

The Wolf von Igel papers, taken by the United States Government at 60 Wall Street, New York, in April 1916, further prove the complicity of the Clan-na-Gael. Casement was captured when he landed from a German submarine on the coast of Kerry, April 21, 1916.

The rebellion broke out in Dublin on Easter Monday, April 24, 1916 and on April 29 P. H. Pearse, the rebel leader, President of the Provisional government, surrendered to General Sir John Maxwell, and on the first of May the rebels surrendered.

After the entry of the United States into the war in 1917, the Irish-German headquarters were transferred to Spain, operating from there via South America back to the Clan-na-Gael.

"In 1921, on the 6th of December, the Irish representatives and the Cabinet signed a Peace Treaty which gave Ireland the status of a Dominion."

For root of this movement see Chapter LXXXII.

For development of this movement see Chapter CXVI.

CHAPTER LXXXIX

THE NIHILISTS
(FOUNDED 1869)

THE NIHILISTS WERE founded in the spring of 1869 by Netchaief who had adopted the views of social organization which have found expression in the works of Proudhon and Abbe Constant.

As anarchists, they embraced the usual anarchist ideals some of which, such as "property is theft", and "death to Tyrants", could be useful to other organizations.

CHAPTER XC

THE CRYPTIC RITE
(FOUNDED IN ENGLAND 1871)

INTRODUCED INTO ENGLAND in 1871 from America under the authority of the Grand Council of New York, the Grand Mastership was awarded by the Grand Council to the Rev. G. R. Portal, M. A., in 1873.

CHAPTER XCI

THE SAT BHAI OF PRAGUE
(FOUNDED 1872)

ACCORDING TO JOHN Yarker, who was president of the order, "this is a Hindu Society organized by the Pundit of an Anglo-Indian regiment, and brought into this country, about the year 1872 by Major J. H. Lawrence Archer. The name alludes to the bird *Malacocercis grisis* which always fly by sevens. It has seven descending degrees, each of seven disciples who constitute their seven and seven ascending degrees of Perfection *Ekata* or Unity. Its object is the study and development of Indian philosophy. Somehow, its raison d'etre ceased to be necessary when the Theosophical Society was established by the late H. P. Blavatsky, which at one time at least had its secret signs of Reception."[85]

References are said to have been made to its esoteric object in Rudyard Kipling's *Kim* which, according to Rene Guenon, can be accepted as a regular autobiography. According to Guenon "that which is told therein concerning the rivalry of the Russians and the English in southern India is strictly historical. Among other things one finds curious details on the organization by the English, for this purpose, of a secret society called Sat Bhai".[86]

For development of this movement see Chapters XCV, CI.

CHAPTER XCII

ANCIENT AND PRIMITIVE RITE
(RITE OF MEMPHIS) (ENGLAND)
(FOUNDED 1872)

JOHN YARKER, IN a pamphlet *The Grand Mystic Temple*, states that in 1872 "we (the English) took from them (the Americans) a Charter for its (The Ancient and Primitive Rite) degrees 33–95 in and for Great Britain and Ireland and in the Scottish Rite allied ourselves with the Supreme Grand Council 33, (Cerneau) for the United States of America, of which the writer (John Yarker) was made honorary 33°, Representative of Amity. We had thus for long the Scottish Rite allied with Mizraim, and now with Memphis. In the case of the former, we established Representatives with various Supreme Grand Councils and revised the Statutes of 1762, in preference to the forged Constitution of 1786 in the year 1884; in Mizraim with the old bodies of Naples and Paris; and in Memphis with America, Egypt, Roumania and various other bodies working that Rite. We also, in these three Rites, accepted foreign Charters to confirm our original powers."

Yarker then makes the following apologia—

"Whatever may be the value assigned to Craft Masonry in this country (England), a Master Mason is held in small esteem abroad Our object in giving our time at our own cost to these degrees is to break with the unmasonic exclusiveness bred of sycophancy and to give every reputable Master Mason a chance of acquiring the high Masonic initiation at a reasonable cost.[87]

Neophytes upon entering a Chapter received the 18th degree of the Ancient and Accepted Rites (Rose Croix) and Ancient and Primitive Rites and 46th of Mizraim. Advanced in a Senate, these receive the 30th of the two Rites and the 66th of Mizraim. In the series of the Council they receive the higher and more important occult grades of Mizraim and Memphis or Ancient and Primitive Masonry.

"The governing body or 'Sovereign-Sanctuary Supreme Grand Council of Rites 33–95 has already issued Charters for Grand Mystic Temples, Council General (of Rites) 32–94, for England, Scotland, Ireland, New Zealand and West Africa and each Charter covers a Grand Consistory 32–93, Ancient and Accepted Rite and Supreme Grand Council, 33rd. It has also established a Sovereign body with like powers for the German Empire.[88]

"The Constitution of the A. and P. Rite declares 'that Great Britain and Ireland derives from the Sovereign Sanctuary for the American Continent, which again derives its authority from the Sovereign Sanctuary of France, the College of Rites and the Grand Orient of France'. In America authority was vested in Harry J. Seymour by Letters Patent granted to him by the Executive Chiefs of the Rite in Paris in 1862. Ten years later a Patent and Dispensation was granted by the Ill. Sov. Gr. M. Gn., Harry J. Seymour, on February 23rd, 1872, to M. I. Bro. John Yarker, as Sov. Gr. M. Gn. 'to establish the Sovereign Sanctuary in and for Great Britain and Ireland;' and he came over to England to inaugurate personally at Manchester and London the foundation of the Rite."[89] "Further on, The Constitution intimates that Egypt was the source of the knowledge deposited in this system. But it apparently arose in France and went to Egypt returning in 1815 with a wealth of esoteric lore, under the name of… Disciples of Memphis."

"None but Master Masons in good standing were and are admitted to the Rite which consequently begins after the three Craft Degrees."

On Nov. 11, 1912, John Yarker was elected Grand Imperial Hierophant 97. After his death on March 20, 1913, a meeting was held at a Special Convocation of the Supreme Sanctuary of the Ancient and Primitive Rite of Masonry at 33 Avenue Studios, 76 Fulham Road, South Kensington, London S. W., on Monday June 30, 1913, at five o'clock, and Bro.

Henry Meyer of 25 Longton Grove, Sydenham, Kent, was elected Sov. Grand Master General for Great Britain and Ireland. The minutes of the meeting were signed by.—

- Henry Meyer 33° 90° 96°—Sovereign Grand Master General
- Edward Aleister Crowley 33° 90° 96°—Patriarch Grand Administrator General
- Wm. Hy. Quilliam 33° 90° 96°—Patriarch Grand Keeper General of the Golden Book.
- Leon Engers-Kennedy 33° 90° 95°—Patriarch Grand Secretary General.
- Theodor Reuss 33° 90° 95°—Sovereign Grand Master General *Ad Vitam* for the German Empire and Grand Inspector General.

The women's branch of this rite and its interlocking possibilities is best shown by the reproduction of Madame Blavatsky's diploma, which was published in *The Theosophist* of March 1913 (M91) and is reproduced again on page 66 of *Freemasonry Universal* Vol. V, Part 2, *Autumn Equinox*, 1929.

There it is stated that "we have declared and proclaimed and by these presents do declare and proclaim our illustrious and enlightened Brother, H. P. Blavatsky, to be an Apprentice, Companion, Perfect Mistress, Sublime Elect Scotch Lady, Grand Elect Chevaliere de Rose Croix, Adonaite Mistress, Perfect Venerable Mistress, and a Crowned Princess of Rite of Adoption."

The diploma is signed

John Yarker 33, Sovereign Grand Master
M. Caspari 33, Grand Chancellor.
A. D. Loewenstark 33, Grand Secretary.

The organ of the order is *Kneph*.

For root of this movement see Chapters XLVII, LXIV.
For development of this movement see Chapter CX.

CHAPTER XCIII

THE ANARCHISTS
(FOUNDED 1872)

ANARCHISTS CLAIM DIRECT descent from Diderot and those factions which during the French Revolution of 1789 had formed the clubs of the *Enrages* and *Hebertistes*. Prudhon was their prototype.

Chronologically speaking, however, the Anarchist party was formed on Sept. 29, 1872, when a split occurred in the ranks of the participants in the Hague Congress of the International Association of Workers, numbers siding with Bakunin whilst others rallied round Karl Marx.

Bakunin's adherents formed the Anarchist party and organized in Switzerland the "Federation Jurassienne" which soon extended its ramifications to Northern Italy, Eastern France and Spain. The Federation's tenets were plainly anarchistic, urging terrorism as the means of overthrowing all forms of existing governments. The attempt of Haedel on the life of the German Emperor Wilhelm in 1878, as well as the murder of the Tzar Alexander II of Russia, 1882, were engineered by anarchists. From Europe, their activities spread to the United States of America when Most, the German anarchist, founder of the Freiheit, went to New York and, with Julius Schwab, organized the Anarchist movement in America, founding the Socialist and Revolutionary Club of New York in 1880 and such press organs as *The Anarchists* of Boston, later followed by *Liberty*.

The methods of these societies are identical with those of the I. W. W., the "Industrial Workers of the World".

For root of this movement see Chapter LXXXV.

For development of this movement see Chapter CXXV.

CHAPTER XCIV

THE ANCIENT AND ARCHAEOLOGICAL
ORDER OF DRUIDS
(FOUNDED 1874)

FOUNDED BY BROS. R. Wentworth Little, W. Hyde Pullen and Thomas Massa, in 1874, this order is restricted to members of the Masonic body only.

Among its members have been W. R. Woodman, M. D., George Kenning, K. R. H. Mackenzie, E. H. Thiellay and S. Rosenthal.

It claims to be a study society for Ancient and Modern Druidism.

For root of this movement see Chapter LXXXVII.

CHAPTER XCV

THE THEOSOPHICAL SOCIETY
(FOUNDED 1875)

THE THEOSOPHICAL SOCIETY, with nine degrees, was founded in 1875 by Helena Petrovna Blavatsky (1831–1891) daughter of Colonel Peter Hahn and granddaughter of General Alexis Hahn von Rottenstern Hahn, of Mecklenburg, Germany, settled in Russia. When very young, she married Niciphore Blavatsky, Councillor of State, from whom she separated after three months.

As regards the founder of this order, Rene Guenon, who has made a close study of Theosophy, thus briefly sketches her career.

"Mme. Blavatsky's extraordinary life of adventure started in 1848. During her travels in. Asia Minor with her friend Countess Kiseleff, she met a Copt (some say a Chaldean) called Paulos Metamon, who claimed to be a magician, and who seems to have been a fairly accomplished conjurer. She continued her travels with this personage with whom she went to Greece and Egypt till her funds gave out, when she returned to Europe."[90]

Having quarreled with her family, she was unable to go to Russia so she went to London where she frequented spiritistic and revolutionary circles. She was initiated into the Carbonari by Mazzini in 1856 and was also an initiate of the Order of the Druses, according to John Yarker.

About this period, (1856) her *Mahatma* Morya is supposed first to have manifested. The *Mahatmas* Morya and Koot Hoomi are said to be members of the highest degree of "The Great White Lodge", that is to say of the occult Hierarchy which, according to the theosophists, secretly governs the world.

Guenon thus continues:[91]

"Towards 1858, Madame Blavatsky decided to return to Russia; she became reconciled with her father, staying with him till 1863 when she went to the Caucasus and met her husband. A little later she was in Italy whither she seemed to have been summoned by a Carbonarist order; in 1866, she was with Garibaldi, whom she accompanied during his expeditions, she fought at Viterbo, then at Mentana, where she was seriously wounded and left on the field as dead; she recovered however and went to Paris for her convalescence. There she remained some time under the influence of a certain Victor Michal, a spiritist-magnetizer. This Michal, a journalist, was a Freemason as was also his friend Rivail (*alias* Allan Kardec) once founder, later director of the Folies-Marigny and the pioneer of French spiritism. It was Michal who developed the mediumistic faculties of Madame Blavatsky... Madame Blavatsky was, at that time, herself a believer in spiritism and claimed to belong to the school of Allan Kardec, from whom she preserved certain ideas, notably those concerning reincarnation." In 1867, she succeeded after three previous attempts in entering Tibet.

"Inquire Within", who acknowledges Guenon as her source of information and who has also closely followed the activities of Madame Blavatsky during this period of her life, refers to her visit to America in the following terms:

"In 1875 Madame Blavatsky was sent from Paris to America where she met Henry Steel Olcott and where on October 20, 1875, a society, said to be for 'spiritualist investigations', was founded in New York." Olcott was President, Felt and Dr. Seth Pancoast vice-presidents, and Madame Blavatsky Secretary. Among other members were William Q. Judge, Charles Sothern, one of the high dignitaries of American Masonry, also for a short time General Albert Pike, Grand Master of the Scottish Rite for the Southern Jurisdiction U. S. A., who was said to be the author of the thirty-three degrees received from the Arabian member of the 'Great School'.[92]

To anyone who has read Part 1 of this book the significance of this connection with Pike and Luciferianism at this period requires no further comment!

Guenon, detailing this American visit of Madame Blavatsky, further explains how "George H. Felt, self-styled Professor of Mathematics and Egyptologist, had been introduced to Madame Blavatsky by a journalist called Stevens. Felt was a member of a secret society generally called by the initials 'H. B. of L.' (Hermetic Brotherhood of Luxor). This society, which played a prominent part in the first stages of spiritistic phenomena in America, is definitely opposed to spiritistic theories, for it teaches that these phenomena are due, not to the spirits of the dead, but to certain forces directed by living men."[93]

Madame Blavatsky and Olcott had both joined this society from which they were expelled before they left America.

A letter from John Yarker quoted in *Freemasonry Universal* (Vol V, part 2 *Autumn Equinox*, 1929) is here relevant. It states that Madame Blavatsky's masonic certificate in the Ancient and Primitive Rite of Masonry was issued in the year 1877.

Yarker writes "Both the Rites of Memphis and Mizraim, as well as the Grand Orient of France, possessed a Branch of Adoptive Masonry, popular in France in the 18th century and of which, in later years, the Duchess of Bourbon held the Rank of Grand Mistress.

"We accordingly sent H. P. B., on the 24/11/77, a Certificate of the highest rank, that of a Crowned Princess 12, said to have been instituted at Saxe in the last quarter of the 18th century."

"In November, 1878", according to 'Inquire Within' ,"Madame Blavatsky and Olcott left for India, and in 1882 founded the Theosophical centre in Adyar, near Madras; there she initiated her 'esoteric section', and contacted the so-called 'Mahatmas', and her phantastic phenomena, precipitated letters, astral bells, materialisations, etc., were in time suspected and exposed. The matter was taken up by the 'Society for

Psychical Research', which in December, 1885, reported her as 'one of the most accomplished, most ingenious, and most interesting impostors.'[94]

"Mrs. Besant was presented to Madame Blavatsky in 1889 by the socialist Herbert Burrows, also member of the Stella Matutina, and she immediately succumbed to Madame Blavatsky's irresistible magnetism and formidable power of suggestion. Madame Blavatsky died in London May 8, 1891. Mrs. Besant was elected President in 1907. From 1910 to its consummation one of her chief works, assisted by Leadbeater, was to train Krishnamurti as Messiah, or as he preferred to be called, 'World Teacher'. On February 19, 1922, an alliance between Mrs. Besant's Co-masonry and the Grand Orient of France was celebrated at the Grand Temple of the *Droit Humain* in Paris."

The Society has over seven hundred affiliated sects at present. "Its objects are, The World Religion, The World University, and the World Government (by the Restoration of the Mysteries, i. e. by the recognition of their place as the World Government as they were recognized in ancient days, the place they have ever continued to occupy...).''[95]

The political status of this organization as a centralizing point for numerous secret and theocratic orders is evidenced by a letter dated July 1, 1926, from 171 Palace Chambers, Westminster, London, according to which the Editors and Correspondents of the English Information Service, to which was given the name of "The Theosophical News Bureau", were officially authorized to issue statements on behalf of:—

- The Theosophical Society
- The Theosophical Educational Trust
- The Theosophical World University[96]
- The Order of the Star in the East (closed)
- The Liberal Catholic Church
- The Order of Universal Co-Freemasonry.

In 1887, when Madame Blavatsky settled in London, she had started a Theosophical magazine called *Lucifer the light-bringer* and published her *Secret Doctrine*. She is the authoress of another well-known work Isis unveiled.

In the year 1889, Mr. MacGregor Mathers, 8th degree Rosicruciana in Anglia, wrote a letter to the editor of *Lucifer* in which he stated that the Theosophical and Rosicrucian Societies entertained very friendly relations[97] and this idea of "friendly foreign relations" is further confirmed by Rene Guenon who writes: "There are persons who believe that the 'Esoteric Section' exists no longer in the Theosophical Society, but that is not so; the truth is that, to defeat curiosity, it has been made into a nominally separate organization but one nevertheless, under the same direction".

The religious principles of The Theosophical Society are gnostic and anti-christian and are the same as those of "The Hermetic Society".

Numerous were the dissensions and many were the offshoots of this association among which the best known are The Anthroposophical Society and The Theosophical Society of America.

For root of this movement see Chapter LXXIV.

For development of this movement see Chapters C, CXXI.

CHAPTER XCVI

PRIMITIVE AND ORIGINAL PHREMASONS
(SWEDEN BORGIAN RITE) (FOUNDED 1876)

KNOWN AS THE Rite of Primitive and Original Phremasons, The Supreme Grand Lodge and Temple of the Swedenborgian Rite received its charter on 1/10/1876 from the Supreme Council of the Phremasons in Canada (founded by the Golden Square Body of London) which was composed of the following well-known Brethren:

- M. N. Brother Colonel W. J. B. McLeod Moore S. G. M., Grand Master of Templars and 33°
- R. W. Brother T. D. Harrington, S. G. S. W., Pt. G. M. of the Grand Lodge of Canada and 33°
- R. W. Brother George Canning Longley. 33°

The officers of the Supreme Council for England then appointed were:—

- M. W. Brother John Yarker. S. G. M.
- R. W. Brother Captain R. G. Irwin. S. G. S. W.
- R. W. Brother Captain Chas. Scott J. P., S. G. J. W.
- Supreme Grand Secretary Dr. K. R. H. Mackenzie.

Upon the death of Scott and the retirement of Irwin, Dr. Wynn West-cott and Major G. Turner were appointed respectively.

All members of the rite of Swedenborg must be Master Masons.

The rite has six degrees, the craft degrees and three others, namely, Enlightened Prince or Green Brother, Sublime Prince or Blue Brother, and Perfect Prince or Red Brother.

The Rosicrucian and Grail grades form the apotheosis of the entire system.

Bro. John Yarker tells us (see page 416 in *The Equinox*, March 1912) that Samuel Beswick informed him that in his book, the matter added by Chastanier had been rejected and "that what was left was the work of Swedenborg. Hence", continues Bro. Yarker, "Bro. Waite's description of two secret and unnamed degrees, are of interest at this point".

In 1902, Brother Yarker, Grand Master of the Rite, authorized Theodore Reuss to found six Holy Grail Lodges in Germany. The officers of this Provincial Grand Lodge of Germania were:

R. W. Theodore Reuss	Prov. Grand Master
Leopold Engel	Prov. Grand Senior Warden
Erich Walter	Prov. Grand Junior Warden
August Weinholtz	Prov. Deputy Grand Master
Max Heilbronner	Prov. Grand Treasurer
Siegmund Miller	Prov. Grand Secretary
Franz Held	Prov. Grand Marshall
Max Suppas	Prov. Grand Steward
Dr. R. Gross	Prov. Grand Steward
George Gierloff, Guardian	

The Secretary of the Sovereign Grand Lodge of Swedenborg in England at this date was Wm. Wynn Westcott.

For root of this movement see Chapter XL.

For development of this movement see Chapter CX.

CHAPTER XCVII

THE NATIONAL LAND LEAGUE
(FOUNDED 1879)

ON OCT. 21, 1879, this organization was established at Dublin, Ireland, with Charles Stewart Parnell as its President. It cooperated closely with the Clan-na-Gael. Among its members were Egan, the treasurer, Biggar, Dillon, J. J. O'Kelly, London and Harris. The league was responsible for many agrarian outrages and in October, Parnell, Sexton, Kelly, Wm. O'Brien and Michael Davitt were arrested and imprisoned. From jail they issued a manifesto advising all tenants to pay no rent. On Oct. 18, 1881 the Government suppressed the Land League.

The American branch of the National Land League was founded in 1880.

For root of this movement see Chapter LXXXVIII.

CHAPTER XCVIII

THE RUSSELLITES
(OR THE INTERNATIONAL BIBLE STUDENTS)
(FOUNDED 1879)

THE INTERNATIONAL BIBLE Student Movement was founded by Charles Taze Russell (1852–1916) with the object chiefly of attracting the lower middle class intelligentsia of Christian communities such as certain clerical workers, teachers, servants and persons not accessible to direct forms of propaganda. In America the movement has had great influence among the negro element.

In 1879 Russell founded *The Watch Tower* of which he was the sole editor.

The Russellite teaching, drawing its own arbitrary conclusions and proclaiming them as final, professes to prove from Biblical sources that all Christian churches are evil and corrupt, that the time of the Gentiles ended in 1914, and that the Jews must henceforth reign supreme over the world. It also elaborates an occult dogma alleged to be based on biblical precedents.

It condemns the Roman Catholic Church, referring to Rome in true esoteric Masonic style as Babylon and disposes of the Pope and his entire hierarchy as agents of the Antichrist who are doomed to extinction according to the familiar Masonic formulas of Albert Pike, Mazzini and Co. We are further told on biblical authority, interpreting the following words in Rev. II. 24 "As they speak" that this means that "Satan is a name applicable to Rome as describing its characteristics."[98]

The Protestant Episcopal and other Christian churches which in Russell's graphic language are "the Harlot daughters of the Romish Church" and "have committed fornication" which term he interprets as meaning the union of Church and State, so bitterly opposed by the Jews in all countries, fare no better at the pen of this prolific writer, who predicts that, under the visible rulership of the Ancient Worthies (The Jewish Sanhedrin), those Gentiles who still believe in Christ will acknowledge his reign as an invisible one while submitting as Christians to all the hardships these Jewish lords might choose to put upon them.

Brother Russell gives us little hope for the time of tribulation which is upon us, for on page 122 of *The Finished Mystery* he wrecks any hopes we might still cherish with regard to benevolent brotherhoods in the following sentence—"As the trouble increases, men will seek, but in vain, for protection in the great rocks and fortresses of society (Freemasonry, Oddfellowship, and Trades Unions, Guilds, Trusts and all societies secular and ecclesiastical) and in the mountains (governments) of the earth".

The publications of The International Bible Students Association are interesting samples of political propaganda and seem well calculated to suppress possible instincts of revolt among such members of the Christian community as might object to the role allotted to them under the Jewish Super State.

The present head of this movement is John Rutherford.

For the root of this movement see Chapter LXXVI.

THE INVINCIBLES
(FOUNDED 1881)

IN HIS HISTORICAL sketch of "The Invincibles", Captain Pollard thus records their foundation and activities: "The Executive of the Irish Invincibles was joined by members of the I. R. B. but the two organizations were kept distinct."

"The Invincibles conceived the idea of assassinating all British officials in Ireland, and held themselves to be guerilla soldiers." Their chief was P. J. Tynan always alluded to as Number 1.[99]

The assassination of Lord Frederick Cavendish, Chief Secretary, and Mr. Burke, known as the "Phoenix Park murders" were perpetrated by this association.

CHAPTER C

SOCIETE THEOSOPHIQUE D'ORIENT ET D'OCCIDENT (FOUNDED 1882)

THE SECRET SOCIETY called *La Société Théosophique d'Orient et d'Occident* was a spiritist organization founded by the Duchesse de Pomar (Lady Caithness) in 1882.

The Duchess was personally in close touch with Eliphas Levi, Mme. Blavatsky, Colonel Olcott, Mrs. Besant, Dr. Encausse, and other well-known occultists of the period.

For the root of this movement see Chapter XCV.

CHAPTER CI

GRAND LAMAISTIC ORDER OF LIGHT
(FRATRES LUCIS)
(FOUNDED 1882)

THIS ORDER, *Fratres Lucis,* was founded in 1882 by an English Jew called Maurice Vidal Portman, an orientalist and a politician who in 1876 was in close contact with Lord Lytton, then Viceroy of India, the author of the well-known occult novel *Zanoni.*[100]

As regards this order, John Yarker, recipient of The Crown of Kether, gives us the following information:

"The Altar is that of Maha Deva and had a ritual of three degrees—Novice, Aspirant, Viator. The writer (John Yarker) arranged with Bro. Portman to amalgamate it with the Sat Bhai, Rite of Perfection, but it seems to be continued separately at Bradford, Yorkshire, as the 'Oriental Order of Light'. Its early certificate adopted the forms of the Cabala, with which the Theosophy of India has some affinity. In the East, ceremonial degrees are not valued, the object being the development of practical occultism, which was the purpose of the establishment of the Order of Light, governed by a Grand Master of the Sacred Crown or Kether of the Cabala. The writer (John Yarker) has a letter from Bro. Portman in which he says; 'the Sat Bhai rituals are without exception the finest and best suited to an occult order of anything I have ever read' and he leaves all arrangements in the writer's hands."[101]

If, as John Yarker says, the Altar is indeed that of Maha Deva, we refer the reader to that part of this book where the Indian cult of Siva (The Destroyer, Maha Deva) is outlined.

The present headquarters of the order are still at Bradford, Yorkshire.

CHAPTER CII

THE AHMADIYYAH SECT
(FOUNDED 1882)

THE AHMADIYYAH SECT is described in an article by Fr. Lawrence as having been founded in 1882 at Quadiam, Punjab, by Mirza Ghulam Ahmad, who died in 1908. It resembles in many ways Bahaism and attempts to conciliate the oriental and occidental religions while its dogma, based on the shi'a (unorthodox Mahometan) foundation of free thought, embraces the buddhist belief, rites and metempsychosis as well as the idea of the occult Messiah.

In accordance with the Ismali theory of the advent of the reincarnated mahdi at the opening of each century, this sect proclaims their founder to have been the reincarnation of Christ for the XIV Century (XX of our era) and the harbinger of the future Messiah.

An Indian branch of the sect endorses a legend according to which Christ, having escaped the Pharisees, died at Srinagar, Kashmir. At this place is the tomb of an obscure buddhist saint Yus-asaf.

The propaganda of the sect is worked from two centres, one at Lahore, India, and the other at Woking, England, the latter being chiefly political in character adhering to the kemalist and panturanic programme.

At Lahore resides the esoteric Indian chief of the sect, Muham-mab-Ali. In London is the other head, Kemalud-Din.

The chief publications of the order are:

The Islamic Review	London
The Sun of Islam	Lahore
The Light Lahore Moslem Sunrise	Chicago
Moslemische Review	Berlin
Revue Islamique	Island of Mauritius

The Durang mosque is attended by English converts as well as Indians. For root of this movement see Chapter XVII.

CO-MASONRY
(ANCIENT AND ACCEPTED SCOTTISH RITES)
(FOUNDED 1892)

SOVEREIGN GRAND MASTER, ELECTED 1929,
THE VERY ILLUSTRIOUS BROTHER LUCIEN LEVI 33°

WE QUOTE THE following from a pamphlet issued under the sanction of the Deputy of the Supreme Council of Universal Co-Masonry for Great Britain and its Dependencies by the Grand Secretary of the said Jurisdiction.

"In the system of the Grand Orient of France the Craft lodges are under the control of the Supreme Council of the highest degree of the rite. The first attempt to found mixed lodges in France was made in 1774. These adoptive lodges spread to other countries, but the modern Co-Masonic Order or, *L'Ordre Maçonnique Mixte International* Was founded in 1882. It consisted of a group of Lodges which united under the name of *La Grande Loge Symbolique Ecossaise de France*, received immediate recognition from the Grand Orient of France.

"In 1872 the Lodge *Le Droit Humain* was founded by Mademoiselle Maria Deraismes in the presence of Dr. Georges Martin, a prominent mason.

"In 1900 the new *Grande Loge Symbolique* amended its policy so as to enable it to extend its ramifications to other countries and to work the higher degrees. Aided by Brethren in possession of the 33rd degree, the body was then raised from a Craft Grand Lodge to a Supreme Council of the Ancient and Accepted Scottish Rites. Madame Marie Martin, the close friend and collaborator of Mademoiselle Deraismes, succeeded upon the death of the latter to the leadership of the movement, (Dr. Georges Martin holding the Office of Grand Orateur) and held it till her death in 1914.

"There are Co-Masonic lodges in France, Belgium, England, Scotland, India, Australia, South Africa, America, Holland, Java, Switzerland and Norway.

"The first English Co-Masonic Lodge was consecrated in London on Sept. 26th 1902 by the Grand Officers of the Supreme Council under the title of Human Duty, No. 6, and Mrs. Annie Besant was created Vice-President Grand Master of the Supreme Council and Deputy for Great Britain and its Dependencies.

"The Grand Lodge of England does not recognize this particular body of Masonry (1927) but Universal Co-Masonry recognises and admits to its lodges Masons of all regularly constituted Masonic orders. Its laws and regulations are based on the principles adopted by the Universal Assembly of Supreme Councils gathered together at Lausanne on Sept. 22nd, 1875."

Much of the real information bearing upon the position of woman in Masonry has been omitted by Masonic writers and the reader would be well advised to refer for it to Vol I.

In *The Hidden Life in Freemasonry* (p. 191) C. W. Leadbeater 33° gives us the following cryptic description of the preparation of the Candidate for Initiation into the degree of Apprentice in the Co-masonic order: "Before his admission he is divested of all m…s and v…s, is h…d, and has his r… a…,]… b… and 1… k… b…, and his r… h… s…d."

"In plain English the foregoing would read: Before his admission he is divested of all metals and valuables, is hoodwinked and has his right arm, left breast and left knee bared and his right heel slip shod."

The candidate thus prepared is saturated with magnetic energy during the ensuing ceremony from which consequently he or she issues already under hypnotic influence.

These hypnotic bonds are further strengthened during the ensuing ceremonies of Apprentice and Master Mason which however, in this order, according to Mr. Leadbeater's description of elementals, undines and other sprites, seem to emulate very closely the phenomena of the Spiritualist's séance room.

After attainment by the Candidate to the third degree the Kundalini is supposed to be fully developed.

CHAPTER CIV

KNIGHTS OF COLUMBUS
(FOUNDED 1882)

THE KNIGHTS OF COLUMBUS is the name of a Roman Catholic organization founded in 1882, in the United States of America, by a Roman Catholic priest, Father P. McGivney of New Haven, Connecticut.

From the Roman Catholic paper, *La Croix*, of Paris, in the number dated December 20, 1913, we gather that, at that date, the Knights of Columbus wielded an immense power with which public authorities had to reckon. Their number then was acknowledged to be more than three hundred thousand. The Order had four degrees and was headed by a Grand Master, six pro-Grand Masters and a General Secretary. The territory of the United States was divided into six provinces, each province administered by one of the six pro-Grand Masters. Each province was in turn subdivided in districts administered by a Master of the 4th degree and appointed by the Grand Masters for a period of two years. Districts were subdivided in councils or chapters.

The *Verité* of Quebec, a Canadian paper, in August 1913, put the number of the councils at 1630. At that time, the Supreme Council of the Knights of Columbus was composed of James O'Flaherty, Martin H. Carmody, William J. McGinley, Daniel J. Callahan and Joseph C. Pelletier.

The order of the Knights of Columbus was the cause of much perturbation in the Roman Catholic Church.

Under cover of being an association for mutual help, it had recruited a considerable number of members who believed that the Order was fully approved by the Church authorities. When however its activities took on the appearance of a Masonic society with initiation rituals, symbolism and secret oaths, many among the Catholic Clergy became alarmed. Their fears were not allayed when it was known that the leaders of the Knights of Columbus were having fraternal exchanges of all kinds with the Oddfellows, Templars and other Masonic bodies. The climax was reached when it was rumoured that in Rome, the Knights of Columbus had petitioned the Pope to allow their members to become, at least in the United States, regular Masons.

The Knights of Columbus, like the Oddfellows, formed lodges of adoption in 1913, women being enrolled under the caption of "Daughters of Isabella". Women lodges were called "courts". In 1913, the number of "courts" was over 200 and the membership of "Daughters of Isabella" over two hundred thousand.

Like the society of Oddfellows and similarly to the O. T. O. of the Rosicrucians the Knights of Columbus hold much power over the property and various interests of their members.

Due to their efforts in the direction of establishing a universal religion and inter-confessionalism, the Knights of Columbus have been considered by a large section of the Roman Catholic clergy as an element having departed from the teachings of the Church of Rome and whose secret aim is to bore from within and disintegrate the Roman Catholic power.

Although the Knights of Columbus and the Daughters of Isabella have extended their ramifications into the United Kingdom, it is in the United States that their strength mainly resides. This is easily understood when one studies the activities of Roman Catholics in America and realises that, there, they are far more a political entity with subversive tendencies than a religious body.

CHRISTIAN SCIENCE
(FOUNDED 1883)

CHRISTIAN SCIENCE WAS founded in 1883.

Mary Baker Eddy, the founder, was born in 1821 at Bow, New Hampshire, U. S. A. and died in 1910.

Having suffered greatly all her life from neurasthenia and hysteria she developed mediumship at an early age. Spiritistic sessions further revealed her psychic gifts but it is more than likely that her early years of experimental psychic research exposed her, in after years, to the horrors of what she later described as "Malicious Animal Magnetism", familiarly referred to by her students as M. A. M.

At the age of 22, she married George Washington Glover, a Freemason and Oddfellow, who took her to live at Charleston, South Carolina, six months later. However he contracted yellow fever while at Wilmington where he died in June 1844.

In 1853, she married Daniel Patterson, a medical practitioner, from whom she was later separated.

In October 1862 she applied for medical assistance to Phineas Parkhurst Quimby (d. 1866) a healer, who had many marvellous cures to his credit. His medical system was based on an understanding of the scientific laws governing the use of hypnotism, mesmerism and suggestion. It is claimed that she derived her system from him.

Her book *Science and Health* was first published in 1875.

In 1877 she married Asa Gilbert Eddy who left her a widow in 1882.

In 1881, she founded the Massachusetts Metaphysical College in Boston and two years later, when the movement was well established, started publishing the *Christian Science Journal*.

On June 13, 1888, the National Christian Science Association held its second annual meeting at Central Music Hall, Chicago. This had been organized as well as advertised by George B. Day, Pastor of the First Church of Christ Scientists, Chicago, and the speech delivered by Mrs. Eddy on the second day of this session was acclaimed by her 4,000 listeners as an inspired oration. In view of the extraordinary pitch of enthusiasm attained by her audience and knowing the practice of "charging" public rooms or halls one is led to ask oneself the question as to whether the assembly hall had been specially "charged" for that particular meeting. Whether Mrs. Eddy herself, like the Sybils of ancient times, was also "inspired" by outside hypnotic influence is another hypothesis to conjure with.

From then on, Mrs. Eddy's religious future was assured. Under her leadership suggestion became indeed the foundation of a religion, a religion in which psychic force, operating under suggestion, accomplishes definite physical results.

Mrs. Eddy's acquaintance with Mrs. Augusta Stetson, another Christian Science leader, had already taken place for, according to E. F. Dakin, author of *Mrs. Eddy* (page 178) "it was at a meeting in a fashionable home on Monument Hill in Charleston that she first met Augusta Stetson, in 1884... She (Mrs. Stetson) had been born of old Puritan stock in Waldoboro, Maine, about 1842. In after life she shrouded her past in mystery, refused to tell her age, and the town records were eventually burned. She grew up as one of five children in a house which her father, Peabody Simmons, carpenter, built with his own hands. When the family moved to another Maine town, Damariscotta, Augusta was organist there in the Methodist church and a singer in the choir. At 24 she married a ship-builder, Frederick Stetson, who was partially an invalid as a result of imprisonment in Libby Prison during the Civil War. As his wife, she went to England where he secured employment with a British shipbuilding firm. Later, he was sent to Bombay, and here she had an opportunity to delve into a subject in which she had an instinctive interest—the oriental philosophies. In these philosophies affirmation and denial play an important role, and a pantheistic God is postulated—a God who is the Universe, whose mind is All, and of whose mind matter, like force, is but one manifestation or expression in the midst of many."

Mrs. Stetson started healing and teaching Mrs. Eddy's system in New York in 1886, later resigning her connection with the Christian Science church in 1909.

One can almost describe this system as emerging clearly out of the realm of occultism, a kind of suggestion or auto-suggestion, whereby practical beneficial results may be induced in a patient by the application of certain occult laws to their personal medical requirements.

Mrs. Eddy's dogma is summed up by Hudson in the following words:

"Matter has no existence. Our bodies are composed of matter, therefore our bodies have no existence.

"It follows of course that disease cannot exist in a non-existent body."[102]

However, regardless of this paradox and the various opinions hitherto expressed about Christian Science, we recognize, while admitting the efficacy of Mrs. Eddy's use of the force of beneficent animal magnetism, that her personal fear of the action of *Malicious Animal Magnetism,* so derided by her theological adversaries, is logical and founded.

These forces operate on sound scientific lines and those who can use the power of suggestion to gain ascendency over a sick person may use it again later for other motives. The danger of such misapplication is not one to be disregarded in calling in a healer, whatever Mrs. Eddy's detractors may say! That danger is real and every student of the occult knows it.

The movement has become popular and has a following among people of wealth who seem to become the easy prey of occultists and charlatans.

The following extract from the *Daily Telegraph* of Dec. 18, 1930, illustrates this;

HARMFUL DEMONSTRATIONS

A warning against the dangers of hypnotism in public has been issued by the Academy of Medicine as the result of an investigation by a special committee. This was set up at the request of the Council of the Meuse Department, which suggested that public experiments in hypnotism should be stopped.

The academy declares that such demonstrations are bound to have a harmful influence. They are likely to excite undesirable curiosity, and, in the case of many sensitive people, to give rise to nervous and psychological trouble. Another grave criticism is that they may lead young people to believe that the exercise of hypnotism may enable them to influence the will and actions of those with who m they come into contact—"which," asserts the report, "is contrary to the truth."

A resolution passed by the academy recommends the forbidding of such displays throughout the country.

CHAPTER CVI

THE FABIAN SOCIETY
(FOUNDED 1883)

THE NOMINAL FOUNDER of The Fabian Society was Thomas Davidson, an idealist who, in the hope of bettering the lot of humanity, organized a debating club the original aim of which was, according to Mr. Pease, author of *The History of the Fabian Society*, "the reconstruction of society on a non-competitive basis with the object of remedying the evils of poverty."[103]

This non-competitive basis meant maintenance for all by the community as a right, regardless of merit.

The club met fortnightly in the drawing rooms of its various members and in 1884 adopted the name "The Fabian Society".

Among those prominent in the movement in its early days were: Frank Podmore, a spiritualist, Percival Chubb, a clerk on the Local Government Board, Edward Pease, Hubert Bland, J. Ramsay Macdonald, later Prime Minister of England, R. B. Haldane, afterwards Lord Haldane, George Bernard Shaw, Sidney Webb, afterwards Lord Passfield, Graham Wallas, William Clarke, a former disciple of Mazzini, Mrs. Annie Besant, then a radical with an office at 63, Fleet Street, who controlled *The Freethought Publishing Co.*, Dr. Pankhurst , husband of the later leader of the Women's Social and Political Union and Mrs. Charlotte M. Wilson who, while retaining her membership in the Fabian Society "devoted herself", so we are told by Mr. Pease, to the Anarchist movement led by Prince Kropotkin and for some years edited the anarchist paper Freedom.

On page 68 of *The History of the Fabian Society* by Edward R. Pease we read:

"In order to avoid a breach with Mrs. Wilson and her Fabian sympathisers, it was resolved to form a Fabian Parliamentary League, which Fabians could join or not as they pleased; its constitution, dated February, 1887, is given in full in Tract No. 41; here it is only necessary to quote one passage which describes the policy of the League and of the Society, a policy of deliberate possibilism:—

"The League will take active part in all general and local elections. Until a fitting opportunity arises for putting forward Socialist candidates to form the nucleus of a Socialist party in Parliament, it will confine itself to supporting those candidates who will go furthest in the direction of Socialism. It will not ally itself absolutely with any political party; it will jealously avoid being made use of for party purposes; and it will be guided in its action by the character, record and pledges of the candidates before the constituencies. In Municipal, School Board, Vestry, and other local elections, the League will, as it finds itself strong enough, run candidates of its own, and by placing trustworthy Socialists on local representative bodies it will endeavour to secure the recognition of the Socialist principle in all the details of local government."…

"The League first faded into a Political Committee of the Society, and then merged silently and painlessly into the general body."

The foregoing is interesting: first,—as showing the original Anarchist connection with Fabian Socialism as we now know it, secondly,—as an example of one of the most usual methods of subverting an existing organization.

An offshoot of the existing organization was here formed, pledged to a policy or policies which might have been repudiated by the parent body. This offshoot being destined to eventual reabsorption into the parent body could thus assure the successful "boring from within" of the old organization.

We are further told by Mr. Pease that in 1888, "a Universities Committee, with Frank Podmore as Secretary for Oxford and G. W. Johnson for Cambridge, had begun the 'permeation' of the Universities, which has always been an important part of the propaganda of the Society".

By 1890, the support of a splendidly organized intelligentsia was assured to the socialist cause with the Fabian Society as its propaganda centre and a number of local Fabian societies were formed. They were succeeded by and merged into branches of the Independent Labour Party.

On page 209 of Mr. Pease's book, we glean some more enlightening information which definitely connects the Fabians with the Jew-captured organization of the old International:

"The International Socialist and Trade Union Congresses, held at intervals of three or four years since 1889, were at first no more than isolated Congresses, arranged by local organizations constituted for the purpose in the preceding year. Each nation voted as one, or at most, as two units, and therefore no limit was placed on the number of delegates; the one delegate from Argentina or Japan consequently held equal voting power to the scores or even hundreds from France or Germany. But gradually the organization was tightened up, and in 1907 a scheme was adopted which gave twenty votes each to the leading nations, and proportionately fewer to the others. Moreover a permanent Bureau was established at Brussels, with Emile Vandervelde, the distinguished leader of the Belgian Socialists, later well known in England as the Ministerial representative of the Belgian Government during the war, as Chairman. In England, where the Socialist and Trade Union forces were divided, it was necessary to constitute a special joint committee in order to raise the British quota of the cost of the Bureau, and to elect and instruct the British delegates. It was decided by the Brussels Bureau that the 20 British votes should be allotted; 10 to the Labour Party, 4 to the I. L. P. (Independent Labour Party) 4 to the British Socialist Party, into which the old S. D. F. (Socialist Democratic Federation) had merged, and 2 to the Fabian Society, and the British Section of the International Socialist Bureau was, and still remains, constituted financially and electorally on that basis."

In the same chapter of his history, Mr. Pease explains that "half of two-thirds of the Fabians belonged also to the I. L. P. and nearly all the I. L. P. leaders were or had been members of the Fabian Society". The I. L. P. was founded in January 1893 by Keir Hardie and Friedrich Engels, the disciple of Karl Marx.

This Independent Labour Party virtually took over the active political work of the Fabian Society, leaving to the parent body it's literary and propaganda status.

At a conference at Leeds in 1899 it was resolved to form a Local Government Information Bureau, to be jointly managed by the I. L. P. and the Fabian Society.

In 1904, Sidney Webb became chairman of the Technical Education Board which up to that date directed all higher education for England. This event, and the concerted working of a group of Fabians within the London County Council, considerably enhanced the opportunities for further socialistic expansion of the Society.

It should be borne in mind that Anarchists and Socialists, while seeming to differ in their social utopian policies, agree on the first step necessary to provoke an economic condition which would enable them to reorganize the world to their liking.

This first step is the destruction of present day civilisation, the good with the bad.

Their aim of Destruction is the same, only the method whereby it is to be effected differs. This effort at destruction accounts for the community of action of Socialists and Anarchists throughout history.

According to the Anarchists: All must be destroyed in order that all may be rebuilt, but, according to the Socialists, the present system will fall of itself by the passage of certain measures into law. These laws, while framed to appeal to popular fancy, once introduced, can be administered in such a way as to operate the International Destruction which is the primary aim of both parties.

Writing of Babeuf and Buonarotti and their abortive conspiracy of 1796, Professor H. J. Laski in *The Socialist Tradition in the French Revolution* states that "the strategy they (the Babouvists) invented has provided ever since the methodology of revolutionary socialism at least in its large outline".

The Fabians form numerous detached societies, committees, study clubs, associations, leagues, schools and what not, in order to gain the support of nonsocialists for such sections of the Socialist programme which might fail to receive public approbation if the connection with the World Socialist-Communist scheme was revealed. Thus the "sucker lists "of capitalistic supporters of socialism are made available for England. The system is the same in America.

Among the societies which owe their origin to Fabian initiative may be mentioned:

The London School of Economics, founded 1895.

The Fabian Research, founded 1912, later known as the Labour Research Bureau.

The Pan-Fabian Organization, founded 1907.

The University Socialist Federation, founded 1912, later known as University Labour Clubs.

The Labour Representation Committee, founded 1900, known after 1906 as The Labour Party.

Among the members of the Fabian Association during the last 30 years we find the following names: Bertrand Russell (now Earl Russell), Professor H. J. Laski, Mrs. Sidney Webb (now Lady Passfield), H. G. Wells (resigned), F. W. Pethick-Lawrence, George Lansbury, Philip Snowden (ex-Chancellor of the Exchequer and Lord Privy Seal) and Mrs. Snowden (now Viscount and Viscountess Snowden), Will Crooks, Sir Sidney Olivier (ex-Secretary of State for India, now Lord Olivier), the late Brig.-Gen. C. B. Thomson (subsequently Lord Thomson, late Secretary of State for Air), Arthur Henderson (ex-Home Secretary) and Noel Buxton.

It is rather interesting to note how many Fabians have found their way to the House of Lords.

Mr. Pease remarks further that after the Labour Party came into office in 1923, "about half the remaining Fabians in Parliament became either Under Secretaries or Parliamentary Private Secretaries to Ministers, all positions of greater or less influence with the Government".

The following extract from the *Evening Standard*, London, May 28, 1931, shows the accuracy of Mr. Pease's statement and will serve to further enlighten our readers as to the full significance of present events.

A 10-YEAR PLAN FOR SOCIALISTS

HOUSE PARTY RESULTS IN CALL FOR CLEARER THINKING
MR. COLE GETS TO WORK
Open Mind On Empire Buying And Preference
From Our Political correspondent.

The Government is to be presented with a brand new policy. Certain ministers are to take part in its preparation.

It is called a "long run" policy, and is planned "for ten years ahead."

Tomorrow evening a group of Socialists and Trade Unionists will begin fashioning the new plan at a meeting to be held at Transport House. The prime movers are Major C. R. Attlee (Postmaster-General), and Mr. G. D. H. Cole.

Sir Stafford Cripps (the Solicitor-General, Mr. Ernest Bevin, and Mr. Noel Baker, M. P. (Mr. Arthur Henderson's Parliamentary Private Secretary) are among those expected to accept the invitation of Major Attlee and Mr. Cole at tomorrow's meeting.

AFTER THE WEEK-END PARTIES

The new policy – or the plan for a new policy – had its origin in a series of house parties held last year at Easton Lodge (the Labour Chequers), when Socialist politicians economist and trades unionists foregathered at week-ends. Out of these meetings grew the new Fabian Research Bureau (of which Major Attlee is chairman and Mr. Cole secretary), which received the official blessing of the Labour movement two months ago and is now established in premises in Abingdon street.

One of the chief ideals of this Society is the extinction of the poor as evidenced by the following extract from The Sunday Express (London) of May 17, 1931.

DON'T GIVE TO THE POOR

They Ought To Be Abolished!

Mr. Bernard Shaw, speaking at Letchworth yesterday, advised the extinction of the poor.

"Never give anything to the poor" he said. "They are useless dangerous, and ought to be abolished, and until this country becomes determined that it shall never again have a poor man or woman or child in it, it will not be a country worth living in."

The best known and cleverest Destructionist laws now on the statute books are those of the Income Tax and the Inheritance Tax. This form of taxation is calculated eventually to precipitate Municipalisation and Nationalisation which also are part of the Fabian scheme for world perfection. This ideal is to be achieved by the gradual expropriation and pauperisation of all classes by systematic, economic pressure, each class to be separately ruined according to the best means available for ruining it. Municipalisation and Nationalisation means control by government, or, in other words, domination by ONE GREAT TRUST.

Is this Socialism?

There is nothing new or extraordinary in this plan for World control by a centralized, Super-Capitalist power.

It is the plan so minutely explained in *The Protocols of the Wise Men of Zion*.

It is the plan of modern Judeo-Masonic Russian Soviet Communism.

It is the plan of Weishaupt's Illuminati and that of International Freemasonry symbolized by the three points of Albert Pike—Destruction, Materialism, Imposition.

One is all and all is one.

It should here be noted that the ta x question is handled no differently by Conservative Governments, when in power, than by Labour or Liberal Governments and it is well known that any Conservative daring to question the Fabian policy of confiscatory taxation would commit immediate political suicide.

The stranglehold of Fabian Babouvism on England may however eventually be mitigated by an international organization of taxpayers combining as a counter revolutionary body. Who knows?

For root of this movement see Chapters LXXXV, XCIII.

For development of this movement see Chapter CXXV.

CHAPTER CVII

GAELIC ATHLETIC ASSOCIATION
(FOUNDED 1884)

FOUNDED BY PARNELL, Michael Cusack and Michael Davitt in 1884. It was related to the Irish movement.

CHAPTER CVIII

HERMETIC SOCIETY
(FOUNDED 1884)

THIS SPIRITISTIC SOCIETY was founded in London on May 9, 1884, by Anna Kingsford and Edward Maitland, both members of the Theosophical Society.

According to R. Guenon, it advocates a Gnostic mixture of Christianity and Buddhism.

For Anna Kingsford, as for Mme Blavatsky, the Christs are beings who have succeeded in developing in themselves certain superior powers latent in all men. This is presumably the "Serpent Power" or Kundalini, the Sex Force. Jesus is not the historical personage Jesus Christ. Jesus is only an initiate, one of "the Christs" incarnating through the ages in different bodies, other incarnations of the "Christ force" having been in the persons of Maitreya Bouddha, Krishna and the various prophets of the other religions.

As a foundation for a Universal World Religion, the idea is a clever one but its consequences are that anyone who makes enough fuss about himself can become a god, thus reducing the idea *ad absurdum*.

This is the principle which when further elaborated leads to the usual Gnostic belief that: "Man is God".

Man being God is thus infallible therefore, as God can "do what he will". This convenient principle leads in turn to an equally convenient code of morals which, unfortunately, eventually leads to the abyss.

Anna Kingsford and her society were in close contact with MacGregor Mathers the head of "Golden Dawn".

The Hermetic Society eventually became known as "The Esoteric Christian Union".[104]

CHAPTER CIX

ORDER OF THE GOLDEN DAWN IN THE OUTER
(FOUNDED 1888)

THIS SOCIETY WAS founded in England in 1888. It admits men and women.

As a branch of Occult Masonry, its esoteric teaching is a blend of modern Tibetan magic and Theosophy. (See Chapters on Lamaism and Theosophy).

In his *History of the Societas Rosicruciana in Anglia*[105] M. W. Supreme Magus Dr. William Wynn Westcott IX, P. M. P. Z., 30°, informs us that "in association with himself and Dr. Woodman", R. W. Frater MacGregor Mathers J. S. M. IX" founded the Isis Urania Temple of the Hermetic Students of the G. D. (Golden Dawn) and that he (Mathers) was then (in 1900) the Chief Adept of the entirely Esoteric Order of the R. R. and A. C. in France, Great Britain and other countries."

Thus the story basing its foundation on the finding, by A. F. A. Wood-ford, of a German manuscript at a bookstall[106] is shown to have been a fabrication calculated presumably to hide the direct connection with the "Societas Rosicruciana in Anglia."

William Wynn Westcott in the above mentioned book gives the following epitome of the Masonic career of Mathers.

"R. W. Frater MacGregor Mathers (Comte MacGregor de Glenstrae), the present Junior Substitute Magus, was admitted to Freemasonry in the

Hengist Lodge at Bournemouth and was an early member of the Correspondence Circle of the Quatuor Coronati Lodge at which he was a frequent speaker before he settled in Paris. He is a very famous occult student, and has contributed several learned lectures to the Metropolitan College. He is the author of the *Kabalah Unveiled, the Tarot Cards, The Key of Solomon the King and The Book of the Sacred Magic of Abra Melin the Mage.*"

Mrs. MacGregor Mathers, the sister of Henri Bergson, the Jewish-French philosopher, received clairvoyantly most of the early teaching still used in the order from the "Hidden Secret Chiefs of the Third Order."[107]

A. E. Waite was an early member of the "Golden Dawn", but at a meeting held at Dr. Felkin's residence in 1903, according to Dr. Felkin's history, "a split occurred, as Waite and his followers denied the existence of the Third Order, refused to have examinations in the inner, objected to all occult work, and said they must work upon purely mystic lines."

In consequence of the split, the old organization of Golden Dawn changed its name to Stella Matutina with Aleister Crowley and William Wynn Westcott at its head while the schismatic order, under A. E. Waite and MacGregor Mathers, the latter a friend of Rudolph Steiner, retained the old name of Golden Dawn.

In 1912, Golden Dawn merged with Stella Matutina.

For root of this movement see Chapter LXXXVII.

For development of this movement see Chapter CXV.

CHAPTER CX

MODERN ILLUMINISM, ANCIENT ORDER OF ORIENTAL TEMPLARS (ORDO TEMPLIS ORIENTIS) (FOUNDED 1895)

Exoteric names: Ancient Order of Oriental Templars, Ordo Templis Orientis; esoteric name: ORDER O Ft O OV.

MODERN ILLUMINISM, AS we know it, was founded by Karl Kellner in 1895. He died in 1905 and was succeeded by Theodore Reuss, the agent of John Yarker.

In 1902, Reuss named William Wynn Westcott as Regent of the Illuminati in England thus establishing the interlocking directorate between Soc. Rosicruciana in Anglia and German Illuminism. This connection is further explained in the article on Societas Rosicruciana in Anglia in Chapter LXXXVII.

According to *The Equinox* Vol III No. 1, 1919, the official organ of both the A. A. (Atlantean Adepts) and the O. T. O. initiates are taught that this latter order is "a body of initiates in whose hands are concentrated the wisdom and knowledge of the following bodies:—

1. The Gnostic Catholic Church.
2. The Order of the Knights of the Holy Ghost.
3. The Order of the Illuminati.

4. The Order of the Temple (Knights Templar).
5. The Order of the Knights of St. John.
6. The Order of the Knights of Malta.
7. The Order of the Knights of the Holy Sepulcher.
8. The Hidden Church of the Holy Grail.
9. The Hermetic Brotherhood of Light.
10. The Holy Order of Rose Croix of Heredom.
11. The Order of the Holy Royal Arch of Enoch.
12. The Antient and Primitive Rite of Masonry (33 degrees).
13. The Rite of Memphis (97 degrees).
14. The Rite of Mizraim (90 degrees).
15. The Antient and Accepted Scottish Rite of Masonry (33 degrees).
16. The Swedenborgian Rite of Masonry.
17. The Order of the Martinists.
18. The Order of the Sat Bhai, and many other orders of equal merit, if of less fame.

It does not include the A. A. with which august body it is, however, in close alliance."

This publication also states that "the dispersion of the original secret wisdom having led to confusion, it was determined by the Chiefs of all these Orders to recombine and centralize their activities, even as white light, divided in a prism, may be recomposed."

"Secret wisdom" in the case of masonic societies of any kind is invariably synonymous with "occult knowledge."

In the case of the O. T. O. the practice of the "secret wisdom" begins with the understanding of the very name of the order.

The book referred to above contains the following information on page 200: "The letters O. T. O. represent the words Ordo Templi Orientis (Order of the Temple of the Orient, or Oriental Templars); *but they have also a secret meaning for initiates.*"

Were we to make a guess at the secret meaning of the O. T. O., we would borrow the words of Godfrey Higgins, the author of *Anacalypsis* and, with him, "penetrate into the Sanctum Sanctorum of the ancient philosophers of India, Egypt, Syria and Greece." There shall we discover the secret meaning of the Order of *To Ov*, Greek term for the emanation of fluid or invisible fire. It is the *To Ov* of neo-platonism of which Godfrey Higgins writes: "I am convinced that the emanation of the *To Ov* was believed to be this fire." The *To Ov* was supposed to be duplicate, then from that to triplicate. From him proceeded the male Logos, and the female Aura or Anima or Holy Ghost in ancient times always female. The *To Ov* was supposed in himself to possess the two principles of Generation. The reader who already knows the meaning of this "fire" otherwise known as Kundalini, sex-force, astral light, etc. will easily understand the phallic hidden meaning of the O. T. O. However, it would hardly be fair to leave such a statement under the classification of either suggestion or assumption. Proof might be demanded and proof therefore is appended.

The Equinox states that "it was Karl Kellner who revived the esoteric organization of the O. T. O. and initiated the plan now happily complete of bringing all occult bodies again under one governance."

In the "Gnostic Mass" printed in the same volume, mention is made, in one of the orisons, of the saints among which are named Karl Kellner and Theodore Reuss.

From notes written by Theodore Reuss himself and from correspondence between him and Karl Kellner, the basic principles of the O. T. O. have become known and bear out the statement that this organization was formed for the express purpose of substituting the phallic religion for Christianity.

The conception of the O. T. O. was far from being original but it was undoubtedly reformed by the two Germans above named.[108] It was no vain boast on the part of the writer in *The Equinox* to name all the orders as concentrated in the O. T. O., for proof has been obtained that both Karl Kellner and Theodore Reuss were, among a host of others, in close masonic relationship with John Yarker, William Wynn Westcott, Supreme Magus of Soc. Rosicruciana in Anglia, a Warden of the Grand Lodge of England, Papus of the Martinists, etc.

Apparently all concurred in the formation of the esoteric doctrine of the Order of Oriental Templars.

In the Bibliotheque Nationale in Paris is filed a document, dated 1917, containing the constitution and certain information concerning the O. T. O. It states that "The Ancient Order of Oriental Templars", an organization formerly known as The Hermetic Brotherhood of Light, has been re-organized and re-constituted.

As evidenced by the Reuss papers, one may gather that the O. T. O. has existed since 1902. Prior to 1917, the official date of its foundation, it was presumably a secret organization, operating under

Ancient and Accepted Scottish Rites, acting, as these papers indicate, as the link between this organization and the various unofficial International occult groups.[109]

The prominent persons connected with this organization at its start were: John Yarker, William Wynn Westcott, Papus, Karl Kellner, Theodore Reuss, MacGregor Mathers, Franz Hartmann and Aleister Crowley.

Apart from its secret phallic doctrine the O. T. O. seeks to unite with a revival of Gnosticism, the study of the Jewish Cabala, Esoteric Lamaism and Indian Yogism. It seeks to extract from their combined doctrines the practical application of Eastern Sorcery and Western Witchcraft, wherein medicine and hypnotism occupy a place of prime importance, serving solely materialistic ends.

The reader can always be referred to the press for descriptions of the practices of the present Chief of the Order who was obliged to leave Italy following an investigation into his magic practices at Cefalú near Palermo in Sicily.

Calling himself "The Master Therion", Aleister Crowley is also known under the name of Frater Perdurabo and, from his own extravagant writings, we know that he looks upon himself as a reincarnation of Eliphas Levi etc. etc.

To give the reader a feeble idea of the perversion of the O. T. O. we quote the following:—"The blood is the life. This simple statement is explained by the Hindus by saying that the blood is the principal vehicle of vital Prana. There is some ground for the belief that there is a definite substance, not isolated as yet, whose presence makes all the difference between live and dead matter.[110]

"It would be unwise to condemn as irrational the practice of those savages who tear the heart and liver from an adversary, and devour them while yet warm. In any case it was the theory of the ancient Magicians, that any living being is a storehouse of energy varying in quantity according to the size and health of the animal, and in quality according to its mental and moral character. At the death of the animal this energy is liberated suddenly.

"The animal should therefore be killed within the Circle, or the Triangle, as the case may be, so that its energy cannot escape. An animal should be selected whose nature accords with that of the ceremony,—thus, by sacrificing a female lamb one would not obtain any appreciate quantity of the fierce energy useful to a Magician who was invoking Mars. In such a case a ram would be more suitable. And this ram should be virgin—the whole potential of its original total energy should not have been diminished in any way. For the highest spiritual working one must accordingly choose that victim which contains the greatest and purest force. A male child of perfect innocence and high intelligence is the most satisfactory and suitable victim. "For evocations it would be more convenient to place the blood of the victim in the Triangle, the idea being that the spirit might obtain from the blood this subtle but physical substance which was the quintessence of its life in such a manner as to enable it to take on a visible and tangible shape.

"Those magicians who object to the use of blood have endeavoured to replace it with incense. For such a purpose the incense of Abramelin may be burnt in large quantities.

"But the bloody sacrifice, though more dangerous, is more efficacious; and for nearly all purposes human sacrifice is the best. The truly great Magician will be able to use his own blood, or possibly that of a disciple, and that without sacrificing the physical life irrevocably."

To such persons as have read in *L'Elue du Dragon*[111] page 43, the description of the first impressions of Clotilde Bersone (Comtesse de Coutanceau) afterwards the Inspiree (Seeress) cf the *Grande Loge des Illuminés de Paris*, the following note by "The Master Therion" will be of interest.—

"It is here desirable to warn the reader against the numerous false orders which have impudently assumed the name of Rosicrucian. The Masonic Societas Rosicruciana is honest and harmless; and makes no false pretences; if its members happen as a rule to be pompous busybodies, enlarging the borders of their phylacteries, and scrupulous about cleaning the outside of the cup and the platter; if the masks of the Officers in their Mysteries suggest the Owl, the Cat, the Parrot, and the Cuckoo, while the Robe of their Chief Magus is a Lion's Skin, that is their affair."[112]

Animal masks referred to above as being used in the mysteries of the Rosicrucian Order are indeed also described by Clotilde Bersone in *L'Elue du Dragon.*

They were a distinctive feature of the Masonic gathering in the Grand Lodge of the *Illumines d'Orienl* at Constantinople at which she claims to have been present.

It is even suggested by Miss Murray in *The Witchcult in Western Europe* that most of the legends of transformations of witches into cats, horses and other animals arose from references by other witches to craft adepts by the costumes and masks these had worn during the witchcraft ceremonies.

Thus again, the witchcraft of the Middle Ages is reflected in the occultism of today.

The philosophical teachings of the O. T. O. seem to be adequately summarized by its leader in the following sentence:[113] "This is in fact the formula of our Magick; we insist that all acts must be equal; that existence asserts the right to exist; that unless evil is a mere term expressing some relation of haphazard hostility between forces equally self-justified, the universe is as inexplicable and impossible as uncompensated action; that the orgies of Bacchus and Pan are no less sacramental than the Masses of Jesus; that the scars of syphilis are sacred and worthy of honour as such."

Eliphas Levi, quoting from the *Oupnek'hat*, the standard Indian book on Magic (*Histoire de la Magie*, p. 76) outlines the same moral code;

"It is permissible to lie in order to facilitate marriage and in order to exalt the virtues of a brahmin or the qualities of a cow.

"God is truth and in him light and darkness are one. He who knows that never lies, for, if he wishes to lie his lie becomes a truth.

"Whatever sin he commits, whatever evil work he does, he is never guilty. Even should he be twice parricide, even though he should have killed a brahmin initiated into the mysteries of the Vedas, whatever he may do, his light is never less, for, says God, 'I am the universal soul, in me are good and evil to correct one another.' He who knows that is never a sinner; he is universal as I am myself."[114]

Is this not the ever recurring dogma of Manichean Dualism?

Every effort is made to attract wealthy people, mostly women, to the "Profess Houses" of the Order of O. T. O. In these centres, where the "Nudity cult" and other eccentricities are cultivated, the victims become quickly amenable to the insinuating suggestions of such as covet their worldly goods.

To enhance its attractiveness to the public, the system is represented as embodying the secret knowledge which leads to all material success. Playing on the egoistical instincts of humanity, the O. T. O. attracts within its orbit all those who, with inordinate ambition and limited capacity, hope in some nebulous way, through the Glorification of self, to save humanity.

There seems no doubt that the head of the O. T. O. is justified in saying that this order reigns above all others as, everything, from political espionage to blackmail may emanate from it.

Like numerous organizations such as Mazdaznans and Rudolf Steiner's Anthroposophism, it lays great stress upon physical culture and rhythmic movements. Pretenses of producing renewed youth and vigour attracts many adepts. Moreover, it promises its initiates the attainment of their ambition and desires. The "Do what thou wilt" applies to this in an ambiguous manner. The inmates of "Fontainebleau", under the hypnotic power of a certain Oriental, said by some to be an Armenian and by others a Jew, have offered the spectacle of automata performing movements, dances etc., under the will of their master. It was even said that under the Avill of this new Svengali, voiceless people sang beautifully and inartistic personalities worked as well as renowned artists and sculptors.

Advertising the accomplishment of such feats attracted many people to Fontainebleau. What actually took place there has several times been revealed before the French law courts and in articles written by erstwhile inmates of this institution.

As to the American house of the same type, the scandalous happenings taking place within its precincts have sometimes been reported in the

Press. Yet to the amazement of a great many, such places as the "Abode of Love" in England, the "House of Rest" at Nyack in America and Gourgief's establishment in Fontainebleau remain undisturbed.

On entering the O. T. O., aspirants must acquiesce in the complete subordination of their "will" to that of "Unknown Superiors". This provision places them entirely in the power of the "Order" and its secret chiefs.

Under occult dominion Art, Music and Politics all tend to the same end: confusion, a calculated and induced confusion: for minds that are confused will *obey and bow to* the hidden masters!

The rule of the Triangle and Ellipse, together with a crude Geometry in modern art, is the rule of Masonry in aesthetics.

Standing before a meaningless Cubist canvas at an art exhibition one day, a puzzled amateur asked "But what does it mean?" To which the painter replied. "It's not a question of what it means, it's a question of what is its effect on the observer."

Consciously or unconsciously the artist spoke the truth. Psychiatrists tell us that this school of insidious humbug is simply an elaboration of the policy of the interruption of ideas leading to total incoherence and madness. "Cubist" art is an effort to produce certain psychic effects obtainable by optical illusion. Beauty has nothing to do with it. The cubist school is not in the realm of art at all. It belongs to that of medicine and psychic science. Those who forget that this devastating fad of *"The Interrupted Idea"* can be extended to music, literature and every other phase of human effort, do so at their peril.

A mind that is positive cannot be controlled. For the purposes of occult dominion minds must therefore be rendered passive and negative in order that control can be achieved. Minds consciously working to a definite end are a power, and power can oppose power for good or for evil. The scheme for world dominion might be doomed by the recognition of this principle alone, but, as it is unfortunately unrecognized, it remains unchallenged.

Destruction, Materialism, Imposition. These are the three points of Albert Pike and they seem to be ruling the world today.

For root of this movement see Chapter XXII

THEOSOPHIGAL SOCIETY OF AMERICA
(FOUNDED 1895)

IN NOVEMBER 1894 William Q. Judge rebelled against Mrs. Besant's domination of The Theosophical Society.

On April 27th, 1895, he and his followers seceded from the Adyar Society and constituted an independent organization under the name "Theosophical Society of America". This organization, which still exists, has its headquarters at Point-Loma, California, It was first presided over by Ernest Hargrove and later by Katherine A. Tingley. It has branches in Sweden and Holland.

Katherine A. Tingley, known to her followers as "The Purple Mother", was in touch with Bro. Theodore Reuss, Magus Supremus in Mundo of the Esoteric Rosicrucians.

This sect it appears, practises Raja Yoga.

Parents desirous of having their children brought up under its aegis must forfeit all their natural rights of inquiry concerning their children's welfare, this prohibition extending even to their right to assist at lessons.

Pupils whose education has been entrusted to the sect are taught to observe absolute secrecy towards their parents as regards matters concerning the school.

Notwithstanding such subversive rules the school is well attended.

For root of this movement see Chapter XCV.

CHAPTER CXII

IRISH SOCIALIST REPUBLICAN PARTY
(FOUNDED 1896)

THIS SOCIETY WAS founded by James Conolly in 1896 and through him became linked with the anarchist terrorist organization known as the Industrial Workers of the World in America. (I. W. W.).

ASSOCIATIONS OF THE 20TH CENTURY

CHAPTER CXIII

THE YOUNG TURK MOVEMENT
(FOUNDED 1900)

NOT TILL 1900, when the Grand Orient virtually took over the Young Turk Party which was composed chiefly of Jews, Greeks and Armenians, did this movement assume a serious aspect.

Vicomte Leon de Poncins in *The Secret Powers behind the Revolution* (page 66) giving the history and origin of the Young Turk Movement adds the following information taken from the Masonic organ of the Grand Orient, The Acacia (October 1908).

"A secret Young Turk council was formed and the whole movement was directed from Salonica.

Salonica, the most Jewish town in Europe—

70,000 Jews out of a population of 100,000—was specially suitable for the purpose. It already contained several Lodges in which the revolutionaries could work without being disturbed. These Lodges are under the protection of European diplomacy and as the Sultan was without weapons against them his fall was inevitable."

He further adds:—

"The Young Turks entered these lodges and met there in order to organize and prepare the revolution. Moreover a great number of the members of the lodges strengthened the secret Young Turk 'Committee of Union and Progress'... On the 1st May, 1909, the representatives of 45 Turkish lodges met in Constantinople and founded the 'Grand Orient Ottoman'.

Mahmoud Orphi Pasha was nominated Grand Master... A short time after a Supreme Council of the Ancient and Accepted Scottish Rites was also founded and recognized by the French and Italian authorities. "To complete this information, we may add that two of the Salonica lodges, those of Macedonia and Labor and Lux were connected with the Grand Orient of Italy and that of Veritas was under the Grand Orient of France.

For root of this movement see Chapters XLI and LIII.

CHAPTER CXIV

THE AMSTERDAM INTERNATIONAL
(FOUNDED 1901)

THE INTERNATIONAL FEDERATION of Trade Unions, not to be confused with The Second International, was founded at Copenhagen in 1901.

It ceased to function during the War, but was reestablished as The Amsterdam International in 1919.

Its objects include the following:

To unite the international working class.

To promote the interests and activities of the trade union movement.

The development of international social legislation. To avert war and combat reaction.

For root of this movement see Chapter LXXXV.

CHAPTER CXV

STELLA MATUTINA
(FOUNDED 1903)

THE FOUNDATION OF Stella Matutina, with Aleister Crowley and Wm. Wynn Westcott at its head, was the result of a split and consequent reorganization of the old *Golden Dawn in the Outer* which occurred in 1903. It admits men and women.

Dr. Felkin, who had been elected one of the three members of the Council governing the Society in 1902 was appointed head of Stella Matutina by Rudolph Steiner in 1912 at which date A. E. Waite's temple, Golden Dawn, received the order to join with it.

Dr. Felkin held this office until 1919.

We are told by "Inquire Within", author of *Lightbearers of Darkness* (page 152) at one time Ruling Chief of the Mother Temple and of the Stella Matutina and R. R. & A. C. that after the oath of Initiation into Stella Matutina has been taken the candidate is terrorised by the following threat… "If thou shalt fail of this thy oath of secrecy, thy blood may be poured out and thy body broken, for heavy is the penalty exacted by the Guardians of the Hidden Knowledge from those who willfully betray their trust."

Its occult teaching is identical with that of Golden Dawn from which it issued and, for some of its shameful practices, the reader must be referred to *Light-bearers of Darkness* by "Inquire Within." It is regrettable that this expose does not take the reader back to the early stages of initiation.

For root of this movement see Chapters LXXXVII, CIX.

CHAPTER CXVI

SINN FEIN
(FOUNDED 1905)

SINN FEIN, AN Irish patriotic organization advocating boycott and passive resistance against England was founded by Arthur Griffiths in 1905. He was succeeded as president in 1917 by Eamon de Valera. By that time the Society was controlled and subsidized by the Clan-na-Gael and Germany.

After the start of the World War in 1914, it asserted itself as the open foe of England.

Richard Dawson in *Red Terror and Green*, page 176, publishes a despatch sent to Count von Bernstorff, the German Ambassador in the United States at that date. The document was marked "very secret" and dated April 18, 1916. It reads as follows:

"Judge Cohalan (of New York, U. S. A.) requests the transmission of the following remarks: The revolution in Ireland can only be successful with the support of Germany: otherwise England will be able to suppress it, even though it be only after a hard struggle. Therefore help is necessary. This should consist principally of aerial attacks on England and a diversion of the fleet simultaneously with the Irish revolution. Then if possible a landing of arms and ammunition in Ireland and possibly some officers from Zeppelins. This would enable the Irish ports to be closed against England. The services of the revolution, therefore, may decide the war."[115]

The part played by the Irish-Roman Catholic church in Irish National and International politics is gathered from the following telegram from Count von Bernstorff to the German Foreign Office.

"The Bishop of Cork having died, there is a sharp contest over the succession. The present Assistant Bishop, Daniel Cohalan, is the choice of the local clergy; but England is using unusual efforts to have—appointed.—is strongly anti-German, although Germany, at our request, released him shortly after the outbreak of war. Assistant-Bishop Cohalan is cousin of Judge Cohalan, and strongly Nationalist and pro-German. He was the intermediary between the insurgent Cork Volunteers and the British military authorities, and publicly exposed the gross breach of faith of the English with the surrendered men. Hence the effort to defeat him through the English Envoy at the Vatican. It would have a great moral effect in Rome if Cohalan were chosen. If Germany can exert any influence to bring about this result it would defeat the English intrigue against her interests."[116]

Dr. Daniel Cohalan was chosen.

Let us repeat that by a close study of the Ancient Order of Hibernians and the Knights of Columbus, one cannot fail to see the control that Freemasonry exercises over the Irish-Roman Catholic church. This, unfortunately, is a phase of the international situation which is generally overlooked.

In an effort to dissociate politics from religion, writers on these subjects have lost sight of the fact that they are viewing a fight between two theocrasies, Roman Catholicism and Freemasonry.

For root of this movement see Chapters LXXXII, LXXXVIII.

CHAPTER CXVII

THE HONOURABLE FRATERNITY
OF ANTIENT MASONRY
(FEMALE LODGES) (FOUNDED 1908)

THIS ORDER, WHICH began its existence as an organization in 1908, thanks to the efforts of the Rev. Geikie Cobb, admitting both men and women on equal terms, no longer accepts men as candidates, deeming their proper place to be in Lodges working under the jurisdiction of the United Grand Lodge of England. It seeks to supplement the work of Grand Lodge.

In 1920, it presented a petition to The Grand Lodge of England for examination with a view to recognition. To have acceded to the request would have been poor policy and, in any case, unnecessary, so Grand Lodge gave the usual answer and the matter ceased to be further discussed.

By 1927, there were 12 Lodges of this order in Great Britain. We know it is the policy of the official body to deny the existence of "real female masonry" and we also know that many English Masons of high rank as well as members of other rites continue to believe that there are no "real" women's lodges.

These lodges, supposed to have no connection with the Co-masonic lodges under the Grand Orient of France are however an offshoot of this body working the first three masonic degrees only.

Mrs. Reginald Halsey, Grand Mistress, died on December 27, 1927.

FEDERAL COUNCIL OF THE CHURCHES
OF CHRIST IN AMERICA
(FOUNDED 1908)

THE "FEDERAL COUNCIL of the Churches of Christ in America" was founded in 1908. Until then it had been the "National Federation of Churches and Christian Workers", founded in 1901.

Its constituent bodies are—

"Baptist Churches North, National Baptist Convention, Free Baptist Churches Christian Church, Churches of God in N. A. (general eldership), Congregational Churches, Disciples of Christ, Friends, Evangelical Synod of N. A., Evangelical Church, Methodist Protestant Church, Methodist Episcopal Church, Methodist Episcopal Church South, African M. E. Church, African M. E. Zion Church, Coloured M. E. Church, Moravian Church, Presbyterian Church in the United States of America, Presbyterian Church in the United States (South) Primitive Methodist Church, National Council of Protestant Episcopal Church, Reformed Church in America, Reformed Church in the United States, Reformed Episcopal Church, Seventh Day Baptist Churches, United Brethren Church, United Presbyterian Church, United Lutheran Church (consultative body)."

Further data from *Twenty Years of Church Federation* by the Federal Council 1929 informs us that the officials of the organization are as follows—

Officials (in part); President, Bishop Francis J. McConnell, Methodist Episcopal; vice president Dr. Ernest H. Cherrington,[117] Methodist Episcopal. Executive Committee (in part); Dr. Ernest H. Cherrington,[118] Methodist Episcopal; Rev. S. Parkes Cadman, Congregational; Rev. F. Scott McBride,[119] United Presbyterian; Bishop James Cannon Jr.[120] Methodist Episcopal South; Bishop Thomas Nicholson,[121]

Methodist Episcopal; Bishop Francis J. McConnell, Methodist Episcopal.

Administrative Committee (in part); Rev. S. Parkes Cadman, Congregational; Bishop James Cannon Jr.[122] Methodist Episcopal South; Bishop Francis J. McConnell, Methodist Episcopal.

Members of Federal Council (in part); Hon. George W. Wickersham, Protestant Episcopal; Bishop Thomas Nicholson,1 Methodist Episcopal; Dr. Ernest H. Cherrington,[123] Methodist Episcopal; Bishop James Cannon, Jr.[124] Methodist Episcopal South.

Most of these officials are also officials of the Anti-saloon League according to the statement of Dr. Ernest H. Cherrington who is reported as saying:—"The league is controlled by the churches."[125]

The chief achievement, so far, of the Federal Council of the Churches of Christ in America, seems to have been the introduction of Prohibition in the United States.

If the general public is unaware of the motives underlying the Prohibition policy of the Federal Council of Churches, it can at any rate judge of its results which are a national calamity for the United States. No surer method could have been devised for the promotion of general subversion and complete disregard of law and order. A summary of the situation created by Prohibition was given by Mr. Ralph Shaw during the Congressional hearings already referred to. He thus expressed himself:

"For the first time in the history of the civilized world, organized violators of the law are being financed—the criminal underworld is being financed, and financed magnificently. Prior to this amendment, the underworld was dependent for its scanty living upon houses of ill fame and the gambling resorts. The saloons, deplorable as they were, were at least observing the law, and they paid taxes to the State. Now the enormous revenues which were formerly paid into the Treasury of the Government and the State is going to the underworld, and it is going by millions.

"Organized society, resenting invasion of the liberty of the individual, is willing to pay any price to destroy the invasion, not so much because organized society wants what it pays for, but in order to show those who have trampled upon the spirit of liberty that they cannot possibly succeed. The result is that millions and millions of dollars are pouring into the coffers of the underworld and making it so powerful financially that it is able to debauch prosecutors, judges, legislators and all the instrumentalities of government."

The truth of these words has been clearly demonstrated in the sensational revelations made lately in the American press. It is not overrating the power of the underworld gangsters to say that they rule the United States for he indeed rules who is able to "debauch prosecutors, judges, legislators and all the instrumentalities of government".

By its fruits shall you judge a tree.

When, in addition to the above one takes into consideration the friendly support the Federal Council of Churches has constantly afforded to the subversive "Civil Liberties Union", one is entitled to look upon this Federation as upon a tree, the fruits of which are a menace to the national welfare.[126]

CHAPTER CXIX

SUFISM
(OCCIDENTAL)
(FOUNDED 1910)

IN HIS HISTORY of Persia, Sir John Malcolm devotes much space to Sufism or Sopheism.

It is supposed to have been the esoteric knowledge of the Mohammedan religion and in the possession of Ali and his successors.

Sufism in Persia dates from A. D. 1500 to 1736 when the kingdom was conquered by Nadir Shah.

Godfrey Higgins, in *Anacalypsis*, concludes that Sufism "is Gnosticism and that if we can discover the one we shall discover the other." He tells us however that their (Sufist) sect has four stages or degrees and that they have "a species of Masonic or Eleusinian initiation from lower to higher degrees."

The subtle metaphysics of Sufism are contained in the Dabistan and their esoteric teaching is centred around the principle of life. It is essentially pantheistic, the soul being an emanation of God's essence.

The teaching of Sufism was introduced by Knayat Khan into the West in 1910.[127] The centre of teaching is at Geneva and a big temple has recently been built at Suresnes near Paris for the numerous proselytes made in France.

Sufism is Islamic Mysticism and adapts itself to all dogmas.

NARODNA ODBRANA
(FOUNDED 1911)

THE NARODNA ODBRANA was founded in 1911 by the well-known Dr. Karl Kramarsch, the organizer of the Panslavic movement. It claimed to be a patriotic Serbian organization pledged to free Serbia from Austrian influence and to achieve specifically the independence of Bosnia and Herzegovina.

Its secret lodge however was closely affiliated to the Crna Ruka (The Black Hand, a terrorist society) and it had absorbed the large and well known Slav organization "Omladina".

"Sokol", a group of physical culture clubs, served as a mask for the wider activities of the Narodna Odbrana in Bosnia and Herzegovina. This was stated as a fact by Cubrilovitch during his trial following the murder of the Austrian Archduke Franz Ferdinand on June 28th, 1914, which precipitated the World War.

The trial for high treason of Vangaluka which lasted from Nov. 15 to the spring of 1916 gives a short idea of the activities of the Narodna Odbrana.

Its aim, the grouping of all the Slav southern states into one federation, could be achieved only through the death of high standing personalities and the revolution of the masses. The master mind of the attempt on the Archduke's life was Radoslav Kazimirovitch, a Freemason, who had prepared the attempt. He had travelled abroad extensively, visited all the

Lodges and had returned with revolvers and bombs. Among the murderers, Sovanovitch, Cabrinovitch and Grabez were Freemasons and Veliko Cubrilovitch was member of Narodna Odbrana and Sokol.

Gabriel Prinzip, a student, a youth of 19, the murderer of the Archduke, was found to have received arms through Major Tankosich, a Freemason and a friend of the Serbian Crown Prince Alexander, His assistant assassin, the bomb-thrower Cabrinovitch, stated openly at his trial that in Masonry, killing was permissible, adding further that the heir to the throne oi Austria had been condemned to death by the Freemasons two years previously but that hitherto, no one had been found to execute the sentence.

The Serbians however could not divulge the secrets of the Serbian Lodge Narodna Odbrana which, in secret alliance with the Crna Ruka had organized the murder of the Archduke, heir to the Austrian throne. The documents concerning the organization of this murder were however made known and available from the diary of the Serbian Major Todorovitch which was found in Loczinka, and it was clearly demonstrated at the trial for high treason of the bomb-thrower Cabrinovitch that the leading personalities of the Narodna Obrana were Freemasons. (Refer *Kolnische Volkzeitung*. Nov. 1914.).

The *Badische Observer* for June 1917 says that it cannot be doubted that the International Lodges (Scottish Rite) must take the full responsibility for the uprising *en masse* of the Brethren in the Lodges and it is therefore responsible for the political propaganda (made against Germany) and also for the murder of the Archduke which was organized in the Lodges.

On the 15th of September, 1912, *La Revue Internationale des Sociétés Secrètes* contained the following lines (page 788).

"Possibly also, some day we will understand the remark made by a Swiss about the Archduke, heir presumptive to the Austrian throne. "He is all right. It is a pity that he has been condemned. He will die on the steps of the throne.""

CHAPTER CXXI

THE ANTHROPOSOPHICAL SOCIETY
(FOUNDED 1913)

THE ANTHROPOSOPHICAL SOCIETY, an offshoot of the Theosophical Society, was founded on Jan 14, 1913 by Rudolph Steiner, who had been secretary of the Theosophical Society of Germany in Berlin since 1902.

Mr. Edouard Schure, the author of the well-known book *Les Grands Inities*, deserted Mrs. Besant and The Theosophical Society at the time of the schism and followed Steiner into the Anthroposophical Society. Later, however, he reverted also to his old allegiance.

Soon after its creation it practically merged with the Theosophical Society.

Steiner was a friend of Dr. Hubbe Schleiden, the Secretary General of the German Theosophical Society and President of several German secret societies, the Druidenorden, Black Templars, Rosicrucians, and Ygdrasil.

The headquarters of the cult and its chief temple "The Goetheaneum" are at Dornach, Switzerland. This building, a crude "Noah's Ark" specimen of architecture, flaunts the symbol of the cult above its main portal, while within its precincts the use of the *iod* as a decorative motif further emphasizes its esoteric phallic dedication.

Anyone perusing *The East in the Light of the West*, by Rudolph Steiner, will find on pages 38 and 119 to 125 a fairly comprehensive sample of the Rosicrucian doctrine of Luciferianism as advocated by this branch of the sect.

Its Christ teaching is the same as that of the Theoscphical Society and The Hermetic Society.

The Anthroposophical Society is developing an extensive educational system for children of all ages. Its principal school, founded in 1919 by Emil Molt, teaching what is known as the Waldorf System,[128] is at Stuttgart, Germany. The Society conducts a school, The New School, at 40 Leigham Court Road, Streatham, London, and contemplates many further acquisitions along these lines.

Space does not permit of further elaboration of the Steiner Educational system which robs the child of its birthright of innocence and ideals to plunge it into the grossest materialism.

Steiner died in 1925 and was succeeded by Karl Unger.

For root of this movement see Chapter XCV.

CHAPTER CXXII

FRIENDS OF IRISH FREEDOM
(FOUNDED 1915)

THIS SOCIETY WAS founded by Judge Cohalan, T. St. John Gaffney, Jeremiah A. O'Leary and Professor Kuno Meyer in 1915 under the auspices of the Clan-na-Gael.

As regards this organization Captain Pollard gives the following facts:—

"T. St. John Gaffney was appointed representative of the Friends of Irish Freedom for Europe. A bureau was established in Stockholm, whither Gaffney repaired, and from there and at Berlin maintained, along with George Chatterton-Hill, close relations between the German Government and the various Irish-American and Sinn Fein organizations..."[129]

CHAPTER CXXIII

THE KNIGHTS OF THE KU-KLUX KLAN
(FOUNDED 1915)

THE PATRIOTIC NATIONALIST Order of the Knights of the Ku-Klux Klan was founded in Georgia on December 4, 1915, by William Joseph Simmons, a Royal Arch Mason and a member of the Great Order of Knight Templars.[130]

The "Imperial Palace" of the "Invisible Empire" is at Atlanta, Georgia.

Under sections 2, 3, 4, 5, 6, 7 and 8 of its charter the following powers were granted the society:[131]

"2. The purpose and object of said corporation is to be purely benevolent and eleemosynary, and there shall be no capital stock or profit or gain to the members thereof.

"3. The principal office and place of business shall be in Fulton County, Ga., but petitioners desire that the corporation shall have the power to issue decrees, edicts, and certificates of organization to subordinate branches of the corporation in this or other States of the United States and elsewhere, whenever the same shall be deemed desirable in the conduct of its business.

"4. The petitioners desire that the society shall have the power to confer an initiative degree in ritualism, fraternal and secret obligations, words, grip, signs, and ceremonies under which there shall be united only white male persons of sound health, good

morals, and high character; and further desire such rights, powers, and privileges as are now extended to the Independent Order
of Odd Fellows, Free and Accepted Order of Masons, Knights
of Pythias, et al., under and by virtue of the laws of the State of
Georgia.

"5. Petitioners desire that there shall be a supreme legislative
body in which shall be vested the power to adopt and amend con-
stitutions and by-laws for the regulation of the general purpose
and welfare of the order and of the subordinate branches of same.

"6. Petitioners desire that the "Imperial Klonvokation"
(supreme legislative body) be composed of the supreme officers
and "Kloppers" (delegates selected by the "klororo" State convention) of the several "realms" (subordinate jurisdiction): and of
such other persons as the constitution and by-laws of the society
may provide.

"7. Petitioners desire that the business of the society shall be
under the control of the "Imperial Wizard"(president), who shall
be amenable in his official administration to the "Imperial Kloncilium" (supreme executive committee, a majority of whom shall
have authority to act and a two-thirds majority power to veto the
official acts of the "Imperial Wizard" (president) in the matters
pertaining to the general welfare of the Society: and to contract
with other members of the society for the purpose of promoting
and conducting its interests and general welfare in any way, manner, or method he may deem proper for the society's progress and
stability, subject to the restrictions of the power of the "Imperial
Wizard"(president) as is heretofore set forth in this paragraph.

"8. Petitioners desire that they shall have the right to adopt a
constitution and by-laws and elect the first Kloncilium (supreme
executive committee), which shall possess all the powers of the
"Imperial Klonvokation" (supreme legislative body) until the first
organization and meeting of that body, and shall fix the number,
title, and terms of officers composing said "Kloncilium" (supreme
legislative committee).

"9. Petitioners desire the right to own separate unto itself and to control the sale of all paraphernalia, regalia, stationery, jewelry, and such…"

The executive committee of the K. K. K. was composed of members selected by Simmons himself who held his position as Imperial Wizard "for life or during good behaviour."[132] As chairman of the advisory board and executive committee of the "kloncilium"[133] he was regarded as the chief power in the order which was to have four degrees. Prior to 1921 however only one of these was in operation.

Among the objects and purposes of the order were the following:[134]

"Article II, Section I. The objects of this order shall be to unite only white male persons, native-born gentile citizens of the United States of America, who owe no allegiance of any nature or degree to any foreign Government, nation, institution, sect, ruler, person, or people; whose morals are good; whose reputations and vocations are respectable; whose habits are exemplary; who are of sound minds and at or above the age of 18 years, under a common oath into a common brotherhood of strict regulations for the purpose of cultivating and promoting real patriotism toward our civil Government; to practice an honorable clannishness towards each other; to exemplify a practical benevolence; to shield the sanctity of the home and the chastity of womanhood; to forever maintain white supremacy; to teach and faithfully inculcate a high spiritual philosophy through an exalted ritualism, and by a practical devotedness to conserve, protect, and maintain the distinctive institutions, rights, privileges, principles, traditions, and ideals of a pure Americanism."

The K. K. K. require the following qualifications for membership:[135]

"Article IV, Section I. The qualification for membership in this order shall be as follows: An applicant must be white male gentile person, a native-born citizen of the United States of America, who owes no allegiance of any nature or degree whatsoever to any foreign Government, nation, institution, sect, ruler, prince, potentate, people, or person; he must be at or above the age of 18 years, of sound mind, good character, of commendable reputation, and respectable vocation, a believer in the tenets of the Christian religion, and whose allegiance, loyalty, and devotion to the Government of the United States of America in all things is unquestionable."

A few years after its foundation "attacks against the klan were originated and started by the *New York World*, which was owned or controlled by a Jew, Mr. Pulitzer."[136]

These attacks ultimately provoked a congressional investigation into the Society during which the details relevant to its organization above given were read into the record. Many charges were brought against the klan on that occasion but none was satisfactorily proved.

After five years of quiet uninterrupted organization, the society, which had adopted for its uniform the white hoods of the Ku-Klux Klan, its ancestor of the reconstruction period of American history, had reached proportions which the subversive element in the United States regarded with great uneasiness.

The Jewish power, in particular, recognized a challenge to its established dominion of American Freemasonry for the K. K. K. constituted an "Imperium in Imperio" in the heart of Judeo-American Freemasonry, a Christian empire sound and free and, as a masonic sect, one refusing to adhere to three of its chief tenets namely; Mongrelization of race, Antichristianity, and Internationalism.

The Great War was over and the new immigrant "Americans" were mostly natives of the different ghettos of Poland, Russia, the Balkan states and Germany. American ideals meant nothing to them. New York City alone numbers over two million Jews in its heterogeneous population and was derisively known by native gentile Americans as "Jew York".

The Americans had realized too late that in the melting pot of Israel Zangwill nothing melted.

The American Jewish Kahal, fully aware of the menace to their peoples from this new nationalist movement, took precautions against it.

With great political dexterity, the whole press concurring, the K. K. K. was pointed out on all sides as the great foe of the Roman Catholic Church and the Roman Catholics of America, falling in with the ideas, recognized the K. K. K. as merely a branch of their old enemy, Freemasonry.

So the Roman Catholics and the Ku-Klux Klan took up the old fight and the Jews looked on, while their two old rivals proceeded to destroy each other. *Divide et Impera!*

For root of this movement see Chapter LXXXVI.

CHAPTER CXXIV

SINN FEIN IN AMERICA
(FOUNDED 1917)

SINN FEIN WAS founded in America by James Larkin and Peter Golden Monteith in 1917.

CHAPTER CXXV

THE THIRD INTERNATIONAL
(COMMUNIST INTERNATIONAL) (FOUNDED 1919)

IN 1917, LEON Trotzky, through the intercession of an agent acting for Mr. Jacob Schiff of the firm of Kuhn, Loeb and Co. of New York, broke through the British blockade and with a cheque on Max Warburg of Hamburg (Mr. Schiff's brother-in-law) started the Bolshevik revolution in Russia.

Few people seem to be aware of the fact that Mr. Jacob Schiff was the head of the Russian Section of the Jewish International World government (Kahal).[137]

The Third International was founded at a Conference held in Moscow from March 2–6, 1919. The Russian Bolsheviks founded the Third or Communist International, sometimes known as the "Komintern".

Mrs. Nesta Webster in *The Socialist Network* (page 44) describes the foundation of this International political subversion centre, in the following words:

"The Manifesto of the Conference, issued on September 8, 1919, calling upon the revolutionaries of the world, whether Socialist, Syndicalist or Anarchist, to unite as soon as possible and form a unified Communist Party, was drafted by a committee consisting of Lenin, Trotsky, Zinoviev, Rakovsky and Fritz Platten. Zinoviev, *alias* Radomislsky, alias Apfelbaum, *alias* Ovse Gershon Aronovitch, was elected President of the Executive Committee. Among those who later formed the Executive were

W. Maclaine and Tom Quelch of the B. S. P., Jack Tanner and J. T. Mur-
phy of the Factory and Works Committee of England, Jacques Sadoul,
A. Rosmer and Delignet for France, L. Fraina and A. Stocklitsky of the
American Communist Party, D. Bilan of the American Communist
Labour Party, the Jewish leader of the Dutch Communists, D. Wynkoop,
whilst the Petrograd Committee of the Russian Communist Part y was
represented by N. Bukharin, V. Vorovsky, G. Klinger and Angelica Bal-
banova". Let no one believe that these people were personalities in the
game. They were agents. Agents only!

"While the Second International was being reconstituted in Geneva
the Red or Third International was holding its Second Congress, which
on July 19, 1920, met at Petrograd, and then continued its sessions in
Moscow from July 23 to August 7.

"This time it was able to call itself a "World Congress", for no less
than thirty-seven countries were represented.[138]

"At this second Congress the attitude of the Komintern was made
clear on two important points: Parliamentarianism and Syndicalism. With
regard to the former, it was frankly stated that the aim of the Communists
was to destroy parliamentarianism, which" has become a democratic form
of the rule of the bourgeoisie.

At the same time Communists should not refrain from participating
in a political campaign on the score that parliament is a bourgeois government institution… The Communist Party enters such institutions not
for the purpose of organization work, but in order to blow up the whole
bourgeois machinery and the parliament itself from within".

"The foundation of the Third International had immensely facilitated
the spread of Bolshevism by providing the Soviet Government with a
camouflage for its activities. No longer could groups or individuals working in co-operation with Moscow be accused of having dealings with a
foreign power, but only with an independent Socialist organization.

"By the end of 1919 the Komintern had spread its tentacles all over
Europe. In December of that year the West European Secretariat of the
Third International, a marvellous organization controlling a network of
smaller organizations, both open and secret, was established at a Con-

ference attended by Great Britain. At a further Conference at Amsterdam in February 1920, it was decided to mark off this Secretariat as a Central European Secretariat, with head-quarters at Vienna (later known colloquially as the D. I. K. I.) and to set up a new Western Secretariat at Amsterdam.

A Southern European Bureau of the Third International and an Eastern Secretariat of Propaganda, comprising the Far East, were established."

In August 1922, the Convention of the Communist Part y of America was raided at Bridgeman, Mich., and numerous revolutionary documents were seized by the United States government.

Manifold requests for the recognition of the Soviet government by the United States of America, were later met by a refusal on the part of the Senate.

We extract the following from:[139]

Hearings before a Subcommittee of the Committee of Foreign relations, United States Senate Sixty-eighth Congress

Senate Resolution 50

Declaring that the Senate of the United States favours the recognition of the Present Soviet Government in Russia

Year 1924

"It is believed that the evidence presented by the Department of State at this hearing has conclusively established three facts; First, the essential unity of the Bolshevik organization known as the Communist Party, so-called Soviet Government, and the Communist International, all of which are controlled by a small group of individuals, technically known as the political bureau of the Russian Communist Party. Second, the spiritual and organic connection between this Moscow group and its agent in this country—the American Communist Party and its legal counterpart, the Worker's Party. Not only are these organizations the creation of Moscow, but the latter has also elaborated their activities. While there may have existed in the United States individuals, and even groups, imbued with Marxist doctrines prior to the advent of the Communist International, the existence of a disciplined party equipped with a program aiming at the overthrow of the institutions of this country by force and violence is due to the intervention of the Bolshevik organization into the domestic political life of the United States. The essential fact is the existence of an organization in the United States created by and completely subservient to a foreign organization striving to overthrow the existing social and political order of this country. Third, the subversive and pernicious activities of the American Communist Party and the Worker's Party and their subordinate and allied organs in the United States are activities resulting from and flowing out of the program elaborated for them by the Moscow group."

These findings of the Senate of the United States were duly brought up before the British Parliament on Monday July 7, 1924 (see Hansard).

They were however disregarded.

The United States alone persevered in its condemnation of the tyrannical rulers of Russia in opposition to European countries which had welcomed The Communist International at Locarno and reinstated its ambassadors as the representatives of the Russian people.

The Third International disseminates its subversive propaganda through the medium of so called commercial organizations such as Amtorg in America and Arcos in England. These organizations operate in conjunction with certain powerful banking institutions.

The Communist International and Soviet Russia stand today as monuments of the Masonic ideal of Destruction—Its organization of the Terror. Materialism—Its assault on Religion. Imposition—Its communist State.

For root of this movement see Chapter LXXXV.

CHAPTER CXXVI

THE FASCISTI
(FOUNDED 1919)

FROM THEIR ACTIVITIES one may assume the Fascisti to be the descendants of the Calderari.

After the European War of 1914 certain banks, conscious of the menace of Satanism, ultimately rechristened Bolshevism, fearing that the monster might get out of hand, selected certain men whose integrity, patriotism and bravery they trusted and, by paying them a stipend, kept the m as a nucleus, ready, when the signal was given, to rally to a leader.

Fascism was founded at Milan on March 23, 1919 and Benito Mussolini became the leader of "the First Fifty-Five".

On October 27, 1922, the Fascisti marched on Rome.

At a meeting convoked previously, seventy-two socialist-bolshevist leaders had been summarily dealt with, thus preparing the way for the Coup d'Etat.

Freemasonry was outlawed in Italy in 1922, and the Grand Master of the Grand Orient of Italy, Domizio Torregiani, was arrested and condemned to five years banishment to the Lipari Islands. A similar fate also awaited Ulisse Bacci, son and namesake of the confidential agent of Crispi, Lemmi and Mazzini forty years ago.

The Fascisti also put an end to the activities of the terrorist society known as the Mafia in 1928 which, two years previously, had received its death blow at a trial involving 280 prisoners and 1600 witnesses.

The following reprint from The *Daily Telegraph* of May 26, 1931, is of interest in this connection:

ITALY'S EXILED FREEMASONS

"SETTLEMENT IN LONDON"

Not Welcomed By Grand Lodge

The Italian Freemasons, suppressed by Mussolini, have sought refuge in England, but Grand Lodge declines to receive them.

Officials of the Grand Orient of Italy in March wrote to the Grand Master of English Freemasons stating that as they had been compel-led to reconstitute themselves outside their own country, they had settled temporarily in London.

They added that they had no Inter. lion of disregarding the tradition of nationality by which Freemasonry was governed or the territorial rights which belonged to the Grand Lodge of England. They also asserted that they had no desire to make use of the sovereignty of the Grand Orient on the territory of the United Kingdom.

"VIEWED WITH SURPRISE"

The Board of General Purposes, in its report to Grand Lodge for the meeting on June 3, says that it has "viewed with surprise" the receipt of this letter, and has sent the following answer:

"The statement in your letter that the Grand Orient of Italy has settled temporarily In London has occasioned considerable surprise. I am instructed to protest against the action of the Grand orient—"

For root of this movement see Chapter LXX.

CHAPTER CXXVII

AMERICAN PROHIBITION
(THE ANTI-SALOON LEAGUE) (1920)

THE EIGHTEENTH AMENDMENT to the Constitution of the United States was passed and became the law of the land in 1920.

The Anti-Saloon League, the organization which thus succeeded in outlawing the use of all wines, spirits and liquors, was founded in 1874 by a group of Oberlin citizens, headed by H. Fairchild, who became its first President.

The suggestion made by F. Scott McBride, General superintendent of the Anti-Saloon League, before the Senate lobby Committee, on May 9, 1930, that the chief protagonist of Prohibition in America, The Anti-Saloon League, was "born of God and will fight on while He leads" precipitated altercations which, seeming ridiculous to some, suddenly brought a hitherto unsuspected factor to the fore, in which the Wet and Dry issue is concerned.

As recorded in the *New York Herald* of May 10, 1930 (Paris Edition), Mr. McBride's remark provoked the following conversation:

"When Mr. McBride, referring to drinking, added, "Those things in the way of the progress of the Kingdom of God must get out of the way", Senator Blain demanded:

"What authority have you for claiming that the Anti-Saloon League is a son of God?"

"The league was born at a prayer meeting in Oberlin."

"Did you get a message from God that He gave birth to your organization?"

"No."

"Then what notice did you receive that this had been a divine conception?"

"The fact that it was born at a prayer-meeting. We never have such a meeting without opening with a religious service, and we are led by the leadership of God just as the activities of the church."

"Oh! So the league dons the cloak of religion!" "We do not don the cloak, it is real religion."

Then Senator Blain, launching into the fray, exclaimed:

"I don't believe that God would approve of some of your practices, and I think your statement is an outrageous and sacrilegious thing. That's how I feel about it!"

To us, attempting to trace the obscure sources of these movements the following question seems relevant. What "mediumistic" instructions were received at that prayer meeting in Oberlin thus to have fanaticised the faithful?

We note that all religious extravagances seem indeed to spring from the same root, namely, the exercise of occult hypnotic influences over the masses to determine any movement whether religious, social or political. That this is so has been clearly demonstrated in the articles which deal with the Moravians, Jansenists, Anabaptists, Mormons, etc. but to be obliged to add Prohibition to this list comes rather as a shock.

In order that the reader may realize that we have a logical reason for putting Prohibition in this category of extravagances we must stress the point of alcohol being recognized by occultists as a deterrent to hypnotic influences.

Thus the annulling of the receptivity of mediums, conscious and unconscious, by the general use of alcohol among the masses, must create serious difficulties to such powers, if such indeed there be, who seek to rule by thought transference and absent suggestion.

Alcoholism, being undoubtedly a menace to the life of any nation, it is natural that the soundest element in the community should wish to fight the spread of such an evil. Thus again, the hidden powers wishing to eliminate the use of Alcohol for their own purposes, found fertile ground on which to sow the seed of dissension.

This explains the creation of the Anti-saloon League which was in effect opposed to the interests of the Catholic church (Vatican) the funds of which, in the United States, had been largely invested in the whisky trust by the Jew Judge, Max Pam of New Orleans. The Roman Catholic Church, had, by this act of its agent, thus been put in the unhappy political position of fostering the evil of the Saloon!

The move was a clever one, for the Saloon was a manifest evil and the saloon had to disappear. Its disappearance was precipitated by the drastic Prohibition law as a consequence of which, not temperance, but the 18th Amendment, is the law of the land today.

The following report of what may indeed be termed a national disaster was given on Feb. 12, 1930, by Hon. George S. Graham, in his opening speech as chairman of the House Committee 71st Congress (U. S. A.) on The Prohibition Amendment.[140]

"The eighteenth amendment and the enforcement law have been tested for 10 years, without satisfactory results. Enforcement has left a train of consequences most deplorable and depressing to every patriot. Killings amounting to over 1,360 have resulted in the last 10 years from enforcement. One hundred and fifty-one citizens were killed by prohibition officers, and 64 agents killed by citizens. In one year there were 77,351 arrests for violations, alleged or real. During the first year under prohibition there were 29,000 cases instituted, and during the last fiscal year there were close to 70,000. Demand for more prisons has been made and new ones ordered, which it is said will not give relief from overcrowding except for a period of 5 years or possibly 10. Prison population has jumped 4 per cent per 100,000 in the last five years. When we add corruption, bribery, demoralization of the citizenry, disrespect for law, bootlegging, and kindred offences, does not such a picture call for the fair dispassionate judgement of men and women, to come together and reason over what remedy can be devised to abate this sad condition?"

Later Mr. Channing Pollock, in his testimony before the Congressional Committee, made the following statements. (Pages 176–178)

"At the most unfortunate and dangerous of all dangerous and unfortunate times, it has bred class hatred, religious hatred, and sectional hatred.

"I know a great deal about the Federal Council of Churches of America and I have worked with them a long time. I know every one of the men mentioned here today very intimately—Doctor Cadman and others. That contempt of public opinion led the saloon keeper to bring about prohibition by continuing to do things no people would stand, and I want to say this, that if these men in the Federal Council of Churches are not careful, they will bring about the abolishment of the church for that same reason. People will not stand that sort of dictation.

I consider the eighteenth amendment the greatest danger in our national existence. Inability to enforce it spells anarchy; ability to enforce it spells despotism. Between the two lies the golden mean of Aristotle, which is good government."

In reading this indictment we are once more forcibly reminded of the three points of Albert Pike:

Mr. Pollock	Albert Pike
Anarchy .Destruction
Destruction of the Church . . . . .Materialism
Despotism . . . . .Imposition.

But meanwhile this "Despotism or Imposition" established by Prohibition is being helped along its destructive career by all the occult groups which furthered the passage of the 18th Amendment.

Among these are The Theosophical Society, Good Templars, Women's Christian Temperance Union, Methodist Board of Temperance and Social Service and a host of others!

The present officials of the Anti-Saloon League (1929) are:[141]

Officials (in part) President, Bishop Thomas Nicholson, Methodist Episcopal; Director Department of Education, Publicity and

Research, Dr. Ernest H. Cherrington, Methodist Episcopal; General superintendent Rev. F. Scott McBride, United Presbyterian.

National executive committee (in part); Secretary, Dr. Ernest H. Cherrington[142] Methodist Episcopal, Bishop James Cannon, Jr. Methodist Episcopal South; Bishop Thomas Nicholson,[143] Methodist Episcopal.

Administrative committee (in part); Bishop Thomas Nicholson,[144] Methodist Episcopal; Bishop James Cannon, Jr,[145] Methodist Episcopal South; Dr. Ernest Cherrington,[146] Methodist Episcopal.

National board of directors (in part); Chairman Bishop Thomas Nicholson,[147] Methodist Episcopal; Hon. Grand M. Hudson, Baptist (Member of Congress from Michigan and was formerly superintendent for Anti-Saloon League in Michigan); Bishop James Cannon, Jr[148] Methodist Episcopal South.

For root of this movement see Chapter CXVIII.

THE AMERICAN CIVIL LIBERTIES UNION
(FOUNDED 1920)

IN 1924, A book by R. M. Whitney called *The Reds in America* made its appearance. The American Civil Liberties Union founded by Upton Sinclair had by that time become an important branch of the Third International so Mr. Whitney gave several pages to a description of its organization and methods. All these would be quoted here were it not that space forbids. Our chief object in including this minor society among those already mentioned is to show the methods whereby Communism is rendered palatable to those whose world it would destroy.

"The American Civil Liberties Union owes its existence to the notorious pacifist organizations of war-time fame, which were presumably financed by German agents in this country working desperately, and for a time successfully, to keep the United States from entering the war. To be sure, in its present form it has existed only since January 12, 1920, when it was formed as an outgrowth and with the merging of various organizations which were developed during the World War, dating from October, 1914, and the members of which were pacifists, defeatists, German agents, radicals of many hues, communists, I. W. W. and Socialists. Among the organizations included in the merger were such pacifist bodies as the American League to Limit Armaments, Emergency Peace Federation, First American Conference for Democracy and Terms of Peace, People's Freedom Union, People's Council of America, American Union against Militarism, League for Amnesty for Political Prisoners, Civil Liberties Bureau, National Civil Liberties Bureau, American Neutral Conference Committees and Legal First Aid Bureau.[149]

"The activities of this organization are extensive. It assists any radical movement through publications of high standing in order to influence public sympathy toward the radical organizations, furnishing attorneys for radical criminals, conscientious objectors and radical or foreign spies, "bores from within" in churches, religious and labour organizations, Women's Clubs, schools and colleges and the American Federation of Labour, in order to spread radical ideas. The union maintains a staff of speakers, investigators and lawyers who are working in all sections of the country. Lawyers are furnished on short notice wherever a radical criminal gets into trouble. A press clipping service is maintained which keeps the organization in close touch with every radical criminal or group of radical criminals in trouble and immediate financial aid, publicity and counsel is offered. Aiding in this service are some 800 co-operating lawyers, and more than a thousand correspondents and investigators, representing 450 weekly labour, farmer and liberal papers with 420 speakers and writers.

"The American Civil Liberties Union was particularly active in aiding the Communists caught in the Bridgman, Mich, raid.

"An office is maintained in Washington with the Federated Press organization to handle matter requiring direct contact with the Government.

"The policies of the organization are determined by the National Committee and the carrying out of them is left to the Executive Committee which meets weekly. "Mr. Whitney quotes the following paragraphs from the 1920 Lusk Committee report concerning the American Civil Liberties Union:

"An examination, however, of the propaganda and agitation which has been carried on in favor of the forceful overthrow of this Government shows that it does not consist of a mere expression of opinion, but invariably advocates measures for its effectuation. In other words, the representatives of revolutionary Socialists, Communists, Anarchists and other groups, state that by doing certain acts this Government may be overthrown and in each instance the agitator urges his hearers or his readers to commit those acts. It is a well settled principle of law that any reasonable man is responsible for the logical and reasonable consequences of his acts and utterances. "While the Constitution of the State of New York guarantees the right of free speech it also contains the warning that the citizen may exercise it" being responsible for the abuse of that right". The effect of the activities of the American Civil Liberties Union is to create in the minds of the ill-informed people the impression that it is un-American to interfere with the activities of those who seek to destroy American institutions. They seek to influence legislators and executives to repeal or veto any act calculated to protect the State or the Federal Government from the attacks of agitators."

After some further analysis this report says:

"The American Civil Liberties Union, in the last analysis, is a supporter of all subversive movements, and its propaganda is detrimental to the interests of the state. It attempts not only to protect crime but to encourage attacks upon our institutions in every form.

"The union is closely identified with groups in practically every city in the country known as 'parlor Bolsheviki'. Speakers are furnished for these dilettante radicals whose influence would amount to little, but for the fact that they can be counted upon for financial contributions to any movement that promises them a thrill. It has been said that many idle men and women become identified with this parlor Bolshevik movement through emotionalism and because it gives them something to think about. Whatever the reason, the Communists and the Civil Liberties Union agitators make use of these groups for financial aid and as means of spreading propaganda.

"It is well known", as Mr. Whitney further explains," that the Workers' party, as a branch of the Communist party, has access to the 'sucker lists' of people who have contributed to the finances of the party in various cities, and besides has 'sucker lists' of its own which are shared by the Communists. The most remarkable feature of these lists is the number of names of prominent people upon them."

Naturally most of the people on these 'sucker lists' have no idea what sort of an organization they are assisting, but their money assists just the same! Hazy notions of helping the poor and downtrodden and bettering the condition of the working classes serve to produce the necessary enthusiasm leading to subscriptions.

Among the persons whose names have appeared as members or officers of this society we name the following: Roger N. Baldwin, Albert De Silver, Scott Nearing and Max Eastman.

For root of this movement see Chapter CXXVII.

THE V. V. V.
(FOUNDED 1920)

VEREINIGUN G VERGEWALTIGTE R VOLKER

THE ORIGIN OF this society is given by Mrs. Webster in *The Surrender of an Empire* (p. 132) in the following terms:

"The League of Oppressed Peoples had been founded in the United States under the name of the 'League of Small and Subject Nationalities' by Dudley Field Malone, attorney for Ludwig Martens, who was afterwards appointed Bolshevist ambassador to the United States by Chicherin. Aleister Crowley, the well-known Satanist, who was then working in the United States for Germany, was connected with this association through one of its agents in America... After the Armistice the society became the 'League of Oppressed Peoples', a name coined by the Germans who had declared themselves to be the champions of the numerous oppressed peoples of the British Empire".

In the archives of certain Secret Services, there is a report stating that John Wesley De Kay, having travelled from Switzerland to Berlin on a German diplomatic passport, had an interview there with Count von Brockdorff-Rantzau, and four members of the Druidenorden of which the direct outcome was the foundation in January 1920 of the V. V. V.

This organization was to operate in a subordinate capacity to the well-known masonic "Druidenorden" and, at a secret meeting held Jan. 14, 1920, a certain Colonel was elected President of the Council. At the same meeting, a council of the League was founded and provision was made for the headquarters, and representatives in every country. It was also further decided that only bonafide accredited representatives in a recognized revolutionary society, with an occasional "Socialist Humanitarian", would be eligible for membership in this council, two representatives being the quota allotted to each member country.

It was further ordered that a secret Inner Council, the very existence of which was to be ignored by the General Council and the members of the League, was to be formed. Five persons composed this secret council of which John De Kay was the President for life.

The Swiss branch of the society was founded on the same day as the German by a colleague of De Kay.

"The Druidenorden" writes Mrs. Webster, "was the concrete expression of the idea… of the 'Eastern School' of German Monarchists, who believed in coming to an understanding with Soviet Russia for the purpose of a war of revenge against the Allies or, failing this, of undermining them by revolutionary propaganda, particularly throughout the British Empire. This section of German Monarchists never ceased to co-operate with the Bolsheviks after Lenin and his companions in the sealed train were sent by them to Russia: and the marvellous organization of Soviet propaganda abroad has been largely attributable to the German as well as the Jewish brains behind it.

"Up till about 1922 the activities of this German group and the Soviet Government were indistinguishable. Radek—alias Sobelssohn—acted as the link between Berlin and Moscow. The Druidenorden, like the Komintern, was internationally organized with lodges in Rome, Milan, Prague, Budapest and ramifications in England, France, Holland, Italy, Algeria, Canada, Egypt, India, Vladivostok and Japan. At the same time it had two important centres in Switzerland—at Zurich and Lugano—under Baron von A. and Baron von D. who co-operated with the Soviet agents in that country by supplying revolutionaries throughout the world with arms, ammunition and propaganda, Bolshevist, pro-German and anti-Entente.

"This inner secret society was behind the Moplah risings in India in 1921, and it was again the Druidenorden that recruited revolutionary Jews in Germany, and passed them through Switzerland via Milan and Genoa to Palestine, in order to stir up feeling against Great Britain."

"There was also a direct connection between the Druidenorden and the I. R. B. (Irish Republican Brotherhood) though relations with Ireland were principally maintained through the V. V. V. and its agents in America."

In 1922 the V. V. V. founded a subsidiary organization: "The League of Oppressed Peoples of the East", calculated to coordinate the activities of various societies such as those of "The Friends of Soviet Russia" and the "Friends of India".

CHAPTER CXXX

JUVENILE FREEMASONRY
(FOUNDED 1920)

IF A NOVICE is not the son of a Freemason he must, according to the rule, be 25 years old; that is to say, he must be the age demanded by the Priesthood before he can become a Mason. The son of a Freemason, however, can obtain a dispensation as regards the age at which he is admitted into the order. It is only necessary for him to be 18 years of age.

According to an article in *Freemasonry Universal*, Vol. I, Part I, June 1925, page 22—"There are two movements in U. S. A., however, particularly worthy of attention. The first is the establishment of two orders, for boys and girls respectively, under the age of 21. These are more or less attached to Masonry, and the Order of De Molay, which is open to boys, and which five years ago consisted of nine members, today has over 1,177 Chapters, with over 125,000 members. The Order of the Rainbow for Girls, which was only started in 1923, now has over 300 Assemblies, with at least 20,000 members, and is increasing by leaps and bounds".

We refrain here from going too closely into the subject of the boy and girl scouts movement leaving it as a suggestion that parents, guardians and teachers of youth would do well to investigate the judeo-masonic allegiance of scout leaders and masters.

CHAPTER CXXXI

THE LEAGUE OF NATIONS
(FOUNDED 1920)

THE LEAGUE OF NATIONS came into being on January 10, 1920, when the Treaty of Versailles, incorporating the first 26 articles of "The Covenant of the League" was ratified.

Cradled in Mazzini's Masonic Young Europe movement, the League and Treaty are the apotheosis of the policy of the old International Committee of London and its satellite societies.

Of these, Mrs. Webster, in her book *The Surrender of an Empire*,[150] gives us the following epitome:

"It was towards 1850 that a modified form of this scheme became known as 'The United States of Europe'. The actual formula seems first to have been used publicly by Victor Hugo in his opening speech to the Peace Congress held in Paris in 1849, but it was not until some years later that it was formally adopted as the slogan of International Socialism.

The impulse came again from the masonic lodges. In 1866, a Freemason named Santallier composed a work on Pacifism for his brother masons which led to the founding of the Union de la Paix, under the presidency of another Freemason, a German Jew named Bielefeld. The movement spread to Switzerland and on September 5, 1867, a further Congress was held. The proceedings were enlivened by a duel between the Constitutionalists and the Socialists, who declared that kings, soldiers—

and some added priests—must be swept away in order to make room for the new Federation of Republics. The Socialists, led by Emile Acollas, won the day. Dupont, Karl Marx's right hand, was invited to represent the First International, of which he was secretary. Longuet, Marx's son-in-law, also attended. It was finally decided to found a "League of Peace and Liberty", with a Franco-German periodical, entitled *Les Etats-Unis de l'Europe*, as its organ. This association, the 'Ligue Internationale de la Paix et de la Liberte', still exists and publishes its paper".

It is small wonder that members of Fabianism should have made themselves the heralds of the idea of the League of Nations. In 1917, Henry Noel Brailsford, helped by Noel Buxton, a noted Fabian, had written a book called *A League of Nations*, in which he outlined its principles and eventual organization. Later, Fabians proudly proclaimed that with the advent of the Labour Party, which was their party, they had gained full control of the League of Nations. But the most outspoken statements on its spirit of internationalism comes from the pen of one of the Founders of Fabianism, George Bernard Shaw.

In April, 1929, the Fabian Society published a tract (No. 226) called *The League of Nations*, in which the noted author gives an account of the strange relations which exist between the members of the respective national governments and those of the international government of the League. Alluding to an incident which took place at Geneva between Mr. Locker Lampson, Under-Secretary to the British Foreign Office, sent by his Government and representing it, and Sir Eric Drummond, permanent Secretary-General of the League at Geneva, George Bernard Shaw writes: "These deciduous members arrive mostly in scandalous ignorance of the obligations already contracted by their Governments to the permanent governing bodies of the League. As party men they are at the opposite pole to the 'good Europeans' of Geneva. As patriots they conceive themselves to be advocates of British national interests (not to say nationalist spies in the international camp) and expect to be supported devotedly by their distinguished fellow-countrymen on the permanent staffs. They are rudely undeceived the moment they begin their crude attempts at sabotage."

Thus the British Jingo Imperialist finds himself writhing in the grip of Sir Eric Drummond whilst the French Poincarist-Militarist takes the full count in the first round from Mr. Albert Thomas...

"This situation, in which the permanent nominees of the constituent governments are thrown into resolute opposition to their deciduous representatives is chronic at Geneva. One of Mr. Albert Thomas's greatest victories there was won over the French Government when he defeated its attempt to exclude agricultural workers from the scope of the Labour Office on the ground that they are not 'industrials'. *The really great thing that is happening at Geneva is the growth of a genuinely international public service, the chiefs of which are ministers in a coalition which is, in effect, an incipient international Government.* In the atmosphere of Geneva patriotism perishes; a patriot there is simply a spy who cannot be shot.

"In short, the League is a school for the new international statesmanship as against the old Foreign Office diplomacy".

The struggle described by Bernard Shaw as taking place at Geneva between the Assembly—or "Hot Air Exchange"—as he terms it, and the Secretariat of the League on the one hand and the International Labour Office on the other is also edifying. The Labour Office, as its offspring, has the blessing of Fabianism and we are informed that together with its friends it is "quite willing to let the Secretariat die a natural death."

How reminiscent of Marxism are all these utterances of one of the notorious disciples of the School of Destruction!

Another aspect of the League of Nations was given by an ardent Zionist—Jessie E. Sampter, who wrote that "the League of Nations is an old Jewish ideal, the ideal of nationalism and internationalism... The Jewish God-ideal implies democracy and internationalism". Further the same author vouchsafed the information that "the solution of self-determination and the recognition of the necessity for a League of Nations to protect small peoples from future aggression have grown in large measure out of the claims of Zionists."[151]

We also know that Lord Robert Cecil, Chairman of the League of Nations Union, in speeches he made in the United States, in favour of the

League, predicted that eventually it would have its seat at Jerusalem. Thus speaking, he was only voicing the Zionist statements which had already been made by Leon Simon in *Studies in Jewish Nationalism.*[152]

Studying the League of Nations under its different aspects we are led to draw the logical conclusion that it is a Judeo-Masonic achievement.

As the embryonic future World Government, destined shortly to be the Central Government of the European Federated States, the League of Nations is at present concerned with two schemes wherewith it will eventually be enabled to enforce its dictates—viz: one, an international army and air force, the other the International Bank which is already aiming at the creation and circulation of an international universal money. Meanwhile, its creators and sponsors are endeavouring to maintain the illusion of Democracy and its manifold benefits whereas, in fact, they have already erected at Geneva a temple to the Autocracy and Tyranny of Internationalism.

CHAPTER CXXXII

TENRI KENJUKAI
(FOUNDED AROUND 1920)

THE TENRI KENJUKAI, a Japanese politico-religious sect, is an offshoot of the main cult known as Tenrikyo, itself dissident from Shintoism, the national religion of Japan.

It is subversive, inasmuch as its adherents object mostly to one of the main tenets of the Japanese religion, namely, the traditional regard held for the Imperial Family.

When, in April 1928; the police discovered several plots for the assassination of members of the Imperial Family and Conservative Statesmen, it came to light that the Communists from Moscow had had, as chief tools, Tenri Kenjukaists.

Numerous arrests were made, including that of the founder of the sect, Aijiro Onishi. His life and behaviour bear a great resemblance to that of the leaders of the O. T. O., of Theodor Reuss, Rudolf Steiner, Aleister Crowley, Gourgieff, as also of Piggott of the "Abode of love" and others.

Like them, Aijiro Onishi exacted a vow of poverty from his adherents who had to turn over to him all their property. With this wealth he had built for himself a beautiful house wherein he lived in great luxury.

Regardless of place, creed or nationality, the same causes produce the same effects, and greed on the one hand and human gullibility of dupes on the other, lead to uniform results.

CHAPTER CXXXIII

BUCHMANISM
(FOUNDED IN 1928)

IN THE SPRING of 1928 much perturbation was caused in educational circles by the discovery that *Buchmanism*, defined by English University authorities as perverted religious mania, had permeated men's as well as women's colleges at Oxford.

Isis, the Oxford undergraduates' weekly, attacked Buchmanism in its leading article in one of its May issues of 1928. On May 17, 1928, the *Daily Telegraph* partly reproduced it in the following article:

"BUCHMANISM"

ATTACK ON OXFORD CULT-RELIGIOUS FERVOUR.

From Our Own Correspondent. Oxford, Wednesday.

The religious cult known as "Buchmanism," which attracted much attention at Oxford last term, is vigorously attacked in today's Issue of *Isis*, the undergraduate weekly.

"In the women's colleges," declares the paper, "Buchmanism" is procuring the worst effects attendant on perverted religious mania."

"The theory of "Buchmanism ", says the leading article, "we do not presume to judge, but the effects of its practice we deplore. Buchmanism. on the surface is almost painfully innocuous; its semi-public meeting, are patronised by several leading Oxford ecclesiastics, and even housed by one Oxford rector; responsible senior members of the University have attended them in a spirit of inquiry, and gone away satisfied that thee reunions, pervaded by the spirit of comradeship and 'uplift,' and punctuated by 'straight' talks and 'informal' prayers, are probably a healthy outlet for surplus religious feeling: and so, no doubt, they are.

"GIGGLES AND FANATICISM"

"These meetings, however, have, roughly the same relation to Buchmanism as a dentist's waiting-room has to the pain the dentist is about to Inflict. Attendance at several of them is a preliminary step to admission to a group, a gathering of perhaps four or five friend, so delightfully informal that it seems uncharitable lo call it clandestine. Here, in an atmosphere hovering between giggles and fanaticism, restraint is flung aside, souls are laid bare by hysterical confession, and, with a fervour which no longer pretends to be religious, the tenets of the doctrine are discussed.

"Now, Buchmanism attributes to Christianity a four-fold foundation on honesty, unselfishness, purity and love. It is worthy of remark that the first two qualities are seldom considered worthy of discussion. Honestly, in fact, is not a conspicuous feature of these proceedings, from which the sceptical are firmly excluded, and in which the perfervid are virtually hoodwinked.

IN WOMEN'S COLLEGES

"In the women's colleges, although the name of its founder is never mentioned Buchmanism has firmly established itself, and is producing the worst effects attendant on perverted religious mania. One of lit adherents has recently been obliged to leave Oxford. In several others devotion to the cult is producing results not usually associated with the practice of Christianity. The authorities appear to be alarmed but remain apathetic. It is time something was done about it.

"Buchmanism is not widespread. Probably, in Oxford, it never will be. We do not wish to exaggerate the danger it represents, but neither do we wish other people to minimize or senora that danger. Its wont effects, though almost impossible to cure, can be prevented. Accordingly we take this opportunity of asking the University authorities to exert the power which is undoubtedly theirs to remove from Oxford those responsible for a phenomenon which would be faintly comic were it not apt to prostate such extremely unpleasant results."

CHAPTER CXXXIV

THE RACKETS
(FOUNDED 1928)

RACKETEERING FINDS A place in this study on Occult Theocrasy because its adepts are the faithful servants of Mammon and their methods of terrorism, intimidation, plunder and murder are analogous to those of the Thugs, worshippers of Siva. Moreover, according to Fred Pasley, author of *Al Capone* and *Muscling In*, racketeering is organized and controlled by the members of the Italian Society, the *Unione Sicilione*, and the *Mafia*, which he calls an invisible government.

Racketeering, as a system for plundering legitimate business, often with the connivance of the police and government officials, has assumed formidable proportions within the last few years.

Mr. Fred. D. Pasley, in his book *Muscling In*, states that "The Rackets" started with Prohibition in the United States.

In 1928, after Mussolini had suppressed the terrorist Sicilian Society known as *The Mafia*, whose members took an oath to "resist Law and defeat Justice", they found a refuge in Chicago, U. S. A. There, through their affiliation with the *Unione Sicilione*, later known as the Italo-American Union, they manoeuvred themselves into a position which enabled them to cooperate with the vice and liquor purveyors of the city on the one side and the political party machines on the other.

To quote Mr. Pasley:[153]

"The *Unione Sicilione* had become a $10,000,000 a year enterprise, supplying the basic ingredient for the synthetic Bourbon, Rye, Scotch, brandy, rum and gin marketed in and around Chicago, and controlling the sale of sugar to the affiliated distillers of the West Side Italian district: Melrose Park, Cicero, and Chicago Heights."

The head of the *Unione*, "… ruled locally as a despot over some 15,000 Sicilians and dominated the councils of the Unione's branches in St. Louis, Detroit, Pittsburgh, Cleveland, Philadelphia and New York City." He was virtually the chief executive in the invisible government, administering the gunman dictatorship of Chicago.

In 1928, the organized gunmen of Chicago seized control of the Chicago Coal Teamsters', Chauffeurs' and Helpers' Union, local No. 704, and the Rackets entered a new phase, that of economic terrorisation by the armed forces of the Underworld.

In 1931, the *New York Times* of November 28 drew the following picture of the gangster situation:

New York City has become the world's capital of the racketeers, who "with the power of Tammany hookups, reinforced with revolver bullets and sawed-off shotgun slugs" are exacting an annual tribute of at least $600,000,000 here, Fred D. Pasley, biographer of Al Capone, asserts in "Muscling In," to be published today by Ives Washburn. Every trade and business organization is racket-ridden, some of the hardest hit groups being dealers in such foodstuffs as artichokes, flour, milk, fish and ice, the garment trades, the building industry and the various branches of transportation, the author declares.

Mr. Pasley's nation-wide survey pays special attention to Chicago and New York. Crime, he reiterates, has become "big business," thoroughly organized in every large American city "with its various racket departments—whether beer, booze, pretzels, gambling, vice or the muscling in on industry and labor unions—as efficiently administered as the units of a great corporation." Instead of diminishing, the power of the racketeers is increasing and "in Chicago, Detroit, Cleveland, Philadelphia, New York and other American cities the gangster with his syndicate is in the racket saddle in 1931 and riding high, wide and handsome."

In Chicago the annual tribute exacted by racketeers amounts to $200,000,000, Mr. Pasley says. The levy in Philadelphia is estimated at $100,000,000, in Detroit $75,000,000, in Los Angeles $50,000,000 and in Cleveland and Pittsburgh S25,000,000 each. The nation's annual crime bill is put at $1,119,000,000.

Asserting that the rise of the racketeer dates from the enactment of prohibition, Mr. Pasley continues:

"Prohibition after twelve years is pouring into the coffers of the Capones, the Maddens, the Gordons and the Duffys something like $3,000,000,000 a year for the financing of their varied enterprises and the maintaining of political relationships. The State laws which they violated with impunity in their criminal operations were ineffective against them, for it was the record that the only convictions obtained, and these at excessive cost, were for violations of a Federal statute namely, income tax evasion."

The author criticizes severely the practice of freeing gangsters on bail while awaiting trial, contending that this allows the racketeer to silence his enemies by murder, to bribe officials, and to use the power of his organization to defeat justice in other ways.

But the term "Racketeering" does not apply only to the deeds of American gangsters.

Besides the underworld vice rings, drug rings, bootleggers and purveyors to the white slave traffic, we must also recognise the existence of Economic and Financial Rackets organized internationally on a huge scale.

To this category belong the International Foreign Exchange and National Credit Ramps operating to control the currencies of various countries for the benefit of a few "Insiders". Foreign Exchange gambling gains are not even taxable and therefore constitute a doubly valuable racket. A banker's racket!

The Stock Exchange Racket, whereby the invested economies of the thrifty are siphoned out of their pockets into those of the "Insiders" is another popular form of business ramp. Stolen property being tax exempt, stock frauds yield a high return. However we do not advocate taxing stock fraud profits, we merely suggest that the law should provide for the punishment of those criminals who operate such transactions.

Then there are the Tax Department, Income and Super Tax Rackets. Should Racketeers gain control of the machinery of government of a country and use its system of taxation as a means of extorting and bleeding the taxpayer, such abuses are none the less a racket! The Income and Super Tax Racket conduces naturally to the extension of the operations of the Stock Exchange fraudulent operator. The poor pay the tax. Sometimes the rich pay it too. In any case, the honest pay for the dishonest.

And what of the law? People often have to wonder, especially in the U. S. A., whether they can always go to law solely on the basis of a just claim. Must they not sometimes consider whether they will not be acting through a lawyer who may have interests which are opposed to their own? And if there should be such a thing as a betrayal, need it always be paid for in money?

Again, we must not overlook the Social Racket, one of the most interesting examples of which is the now famous "Douglas-Pennant Case". From recent developments, however, it would seem that this was largely a Masonic intrigue. The Chairman of the House of Lords Committee trying the case was the late Lord Kintore, a noted Freemason. Others connected with the conspiracy to ruin Miss Violet Douglas-Pennant's life and reputation were also Freemasons. Nothing was ever proved against this lady and she herself makes no mystery of the fact that she was, for a short time, a member of a masonic organization, "The G. D." She resigned her membership in this body, however, shortly after her initiation but from then onward was hounded and threatened in every way. That her failure to gain Justice in an English court is only a part of a policy of persecution will surprise few of those who have followed her case.

The present wave of International Unemployment is interesting as an Economic Racket. Already France, England and the U. S. A. have been led to segregate their own workers and exclude foreign labour. This course seemed a patriotic necessity at the outset but the idea, exploited to its logical conclusion, spells slavery of the workers. Nations decreeing that only native labour can be employed within their boundaries thus subtly rob labour of its freedom to work where it commands the highest price and best conditions.

Labour, robbed of its right to control its own market, may suddenly find itself restricted to even county boundaries. In that event a condition will arise for which there is already an historical precedent. Boris Goudounoff, through the creation of just such a situation in Russia, instituted serfdom in a country where, previously, the workers had been free men.

Italy, Australia and England have already enforced virtual embargoes on capital—why not therefore embargoes on labour?

The Rackets are the last stage of the battle in the economic war between Predatory Capitalism and Predatory Labour against Constructive Capitalism and Constructive Labour. The progressive stages of this war are outlined in a document known as *The Protocols of the Wise Men of Zion*.[154] The full significance of this record should have been made the subject of a comprehensive course of studies in every school, church and university, but whereas Marxism, which is but one of the means devised for the accomplishment of the *Protocols*, is freely taught and practised, a wall of silence and fear has been built around the *Protocols* themselves.

CHAPTER CXXXV

THE NEW HISTORY SOCIETY
(FOUNDED 1930)

THIS SOCIETY WAS founded on April 5, 1930, at a meeting at The Park Lane Hotel, New York, presided over by Mirza Ahmed Sohrab who read a resolution embodying the ideals of Professor Einstein and Arthur Henderson which was unanimously adopted.

In *Torchbearers* (p. 32), a pamphlet published by The New History Society in 1931, we read that Mr. Einstein has declared the position he will take in the next war; "I should unconditionally refuse every direct or indirect war service and try to induce my friends to take the same stand, and this independently of any critical opinion of the causes of the war."

History is, or should be, the truth on past events. When it is distortion of past records to suit the aims and convenience of specific groups it is not history. There can be no such thing as New History. We are therefore entitled to question the historical basis of this society whose members are the "advocates of the Universal Principles of Baha'u' llah and spreaders of the Ideals of Abdul Baha."[155]

The direct result of another Mass meeting held on April 5 under the auspices of this society was the affiliation of twenty Peace Societies under the name of "Youth Peace Federation".

Among the members of this New History Society we find the name of Besanta Koomar Roy.

CHAPTER CXXXVI

THE YOUTH PEACE FEDERATION
(FOUNDED 1930)

EARLY IN THE 20th Century the headquarters of *The Worker*, the Communist weekly, were at 8 East 10th Street, New York. It also harboured a "Youth Movement" imported from Germany.

In a pamphlet issued by the Massachusetts Public Interest League, (210 Newbury Street, Boston, Mass. April 1925) we read that this "Youth Movement" was sponsored by The National Student Forum, an organization "made up of those elements in the colleges which have at different times called themselves Inter-collegiate Socialist Societies, Liberal Leagues and Leagues for Industrial Democracy. It was Lenin's cleverness which suggested 'frequent changes of name' to radical organizations. This bewilders the public and the new names serve as an alias."

An article in the *Survey Graphic* for December 1921 stated the aims of this movement to include advocation of the Nudity Cult and promiscuity in sex relationships under the name of free love. Its advocacy of Body worship enables us to classify it as "Phallic". "It is the purpose of the National Student Forum", writes R. M. Whitney, in a pamphlet entitled *The Youth movement*, "and the other organizations which it supports by its sympathy, to undermine and sink, or overthrow, the Government of the United States, and to set up in this country a soviet form of government, such as Russia now boasts."

"Its constituent organizations are:

Barnard Social Science Club.
Bryn Mawr Liberal Club.
Dartmouth Round Table.
George Washington University Free Lance Club.
Harvard Student Liberal Club.
Hood College Contemporary Club.
Hollins (Virginia) Student Forum.
Howard (coloured) Student Progressive Club.
Mt. Holyoke Forum.
Miami University Law School Liberal Club.
Northwestern University Liberal League.
Oberlin College Liberal Club.
Park College Social Science Club.
Rockford College International Relations Club.
Radcliffe Liberal Club.
Stanford University Forum.
Swarthmore Polity Club.
University of Chicago Liberal Club.
University of Colorado Forum.
Union Theological Seminary Contemporary Club.
Vassar College Political Association.
Wellesley College Forum.
Western College Forum.
Yale Liberal Club". [156]

The first executive Secretary of the National Student Forum was Mr. John Rothschild, a New York Socialist. Among others interested in the movement was

"W. A. Robeson, an Englishman who had studied under Harold Laski, the Radical who came into the limelight while teaching at Harvard." [157] Robeson was a member of the Advisory Committee of the British Labour Party and a friend of the well-known Fabian, Mr. George Bernard Shaw.

In the *New Student*, the organ of the National Student Forum of Dec. 2nd, 1922, Mr. George Bernard Shaw is quoted as saying;—"A s far as I can gather, if the students in American Universities do not organize their own education, they will not get any. The professors are overworked schoolmasters, underpaid, and deprived of all liberty of speech and conscience. From them nothing can be expected… the remedy is cooperative organization by the consumers; that is, by the students… In forming intellectual Soviets, and establishing the Dictatorship of the Learner, the American students may save their country, if it is capable of being saved. If not, they will at least learn something, and perhaps teach something, in the *ecstasy of demolition*."

In a speech made in Moscow in June, 1923, Zinovieff (Chairman of The Young Communist International Movement) said:—"The Youth Movement is the best section of the Communist International."[158]

In further corroboration of the tendencies of this organisation to an "ecstasy of demolition", Professor George Leiken of the Volga region is further mentioned in the pamphlet above referred to as saying:—"When the Russian youth reaches the age of 12 the so-called League of Communist Youth awaits him. This organization accepts girls as well as boys and promptly reduces them to a low state of moral corruption. The institutions of marriage and home are ignored…

"Children are taught that they owe no obedience to parents, that they need acknowledge no authority but the Red Government."

"It was W. Z. Foster, one of Moscow's cleverest agents, who said: 'Communists get things done and paid for by others'."

The Youth Peace Federation founded in 1930 is also to be found at 8 East 10th Street, New York. Organized in April 14 1930 at the residence oi Mr. and Mrs. Lewis Stuyvesant Chanler this society was founded at a mass meeting held under the auspices of "The New History Society" on April 5, 1931. It is the collective name of the following associations:—

- Civic Club, Junior Group;
- International Club;
- League of Youth of Community Church;

- Methodist Epworth League, New York District;
- New York Committee of the Fellowship of Reconciliation;
- Pioneer Youth of America;
- Progressive Youth League of Bronx Free Fellowship;
- Seven Arts Club;
- The Peace Education Group of the Ethical Culture Society of New York;
- Women's International League for Peace and Freedom (Junior Group);
- Women's Peace Society (Junior Group); Young Caravan;
- Young Circle League;
- Young Judea;
- Young Peoples Fellowship of St. Philip's Parish (Senior);
- Young Peoples Fellowship of St. Philip's Parish (Junior);
- Young Peoples Group of the Ethical Culture Society, Brooklyn, N. Y.
- Young Peoples Socialist League of Greater New York;
- Young Poale Zion;
- Youth Section of the War Resisters League.[159]

The above organization is that familiar to any business man of a Holding Corporation in which are joined subsidiary companies.

Basing our deductions on the foregoing articles in this book we conclude that the secret objectives of this corporation may be:

Disarmament of all countries except Russia in order to facilitate the rule of the World by the International Jewish Super-Capitalist Group now dominating Russia with the Red Army under its control, and the end of Democracy.

A basic principle of war strategy is to have your enemy unprepared for assault.

The Massachusetts Public Interest League warns us that:

"The Youth Movement is using American Youth as a pawn in the Communist game.

The real menace of the movement in this country (America) lies in the fact that it is revolutionary propaganda in romantic disguise subtly preaching to immature youth the *ecstasy of demolition* of the foundations of civilization."

CHAPTER CXXXVII

THE INTERNATIONAL BANK
(FOUNDED 1930)

THE INTERNATIONALIZATION OF finance reached its apotheosis when, on April 23, 1930 the International Bank at Basle, commissioned to enroll the central banks of nine nations in its membership, was founded.

As for the delegates from the different countries attending the meeting their names signify little for, owing to the speed and unanimity with which official appointments were made, it is evident that they were all instructed, or, in other words pledged, to obey orders. By whom were the orders given? History may answer that question some day!

Mr. Gates McGarrah was elected chairman of the board of directors with Mr. Leon Frazer his deputy and Sir Charles Addis and Dr. Melchior were elected vice-chairmen.

The significance of this international institution was commented upon in an article entitled "Mammon being enthroned" by "Arthurian" in the *Referee* dated Sunday, April 13, 1930, in the following terms which, while constituting a warning to the English people, is actually an appeal to the people of the world. "One is amazed at the equanimity with which Sir Charles Addis describes the difficulty of enabling the Bank for International Settlements to avoid interference with the Sovereign Rights of the people of each of so many countries! Surely the possibility alone ought to be adequate condemnation of the bank. The opening for chicanery,

brute force, bribery, corruption and war, in the supposed solution of this
problem, is unprecedented in the history of the world

"The Bank is to exist for fifty years, if it can; it is to pay no taxes during
all that time; and its assets and deposits are to be immune from seizure,
confiscation, and censorship, in peace or war; it is also to be subject to no
restriction or prohibition of any kind on its imports and exports of gold
or currency. So little do Government decisions regarding the Bank really
count that, before the scheme has been sanctioned, the first part of the
subscription has already been subscribed. The Bankers and business men
to be associated are to ensure that there will be no uncertainty about the
business that the Bank will promote, the 'money troubles which lie at the
root' of the industrial depression and financial uncertainty are, of course,
going to be cured by them—so they say. The Governor of the Bank of
England (Mr. Montagu Norman) is going to be a director of this foreign
Bank. What an honour! This Board, with the daily lives of hundreds of
millions of people at its mercy, is going to meet at least ten times a year—
four times at Basle...

'The Bank owes allegiance to no single Government.' It need keep no
currency reserve...

"This Bank that owes no allegiance to anyone can do as it likes, Mammon is enthroned upon the world, to make what profits it can, with unre-
stricted powers, for fifty years! In addition to its extraordinary powers, it
has control of the 'Machinery of Reparations' which contains the means
by which the wherewithal to liquidate Reparations can be squeezed out of
the receivers at a profit to the payers... Economic control involves political control as well as every other control of any people. Truly, the megalo-
mania of finance never went further, truly, there has never been anything
like it in the world before

"People of England! Remember how the stranglehold of the Rank of
England on all the other banks, on all the other financial houses, upon
every business and upon every home and family has grown from the com-
paratively negligible sum of £1,200,000 of similar credit free of interest
and the 'usufruct' thereof. This new usufruct will be the impoverishment,
debasement, extinction, and disintegration of all that the masses of this

country care for, and the certain decline and fall and redistribution, into foreign hands, of the British Empire… "In this country we have asked for the creation of interest-free credit to be lent to the people to be used for the production of wealth by and for the people, but by a great conspiracy of silence the idea is being suppressed. The hidden prize is not intended for us. Only those who have been swindled on a race-course by three-card trick men can realize what is now being done to all the peoples of the Allied countries by a debased money and credit-upon-credit trick, the like of which has never been attempted in the world before…

"The alleged £80,000,000 per annum that Germany is supposed to pay to the United States for fifty-nine years is a delusion and a snare. But the aim of the section of Wall Street repudiated by President Hoover, which initially promoted the idea of the Plan (The Young Plan), is that , through Germany, this section of Wall Street shall dominate the world."

Note: Compare with The Protocols, (L. Fry, op. cit.)

CONCLUSION

THE FOREGOING PAGES have had for object to show how, whether open or secret, a great many societies, masonic and non-masonic, of good or evil intent, seem to function towards the same goal under centralized leadership.

This book claims to be an endeavour to prove that:—

1—*Owing to their union,* all secret societies, whether political, philanthropic or occult in appearance, serve a political purpose unknown to the majority of their members.
2—The power wielded by such societies is real and its character is international.
3—Regardless of their exoteric objects, the esoteric aims of most societies are all directed towards the same end—namely: the concentration of political, economic and intellectual power into the hands of a small group of individuals, each of whom controls a branch of the International life, material and spiritual, of the world today.

The main branches thus controlled are:—

1—The International Banking Groups and their subsidiaries.
2—International, industrial and commercial control groups with their interlocking directorates.
3—Education, Art, Literature, Science, and Religion. as vehicles of intellectual and moral perversion.
4—The Groups already organized throughout different countries for the study of International affairs political, financial and economic.
5—The International Press, the medium used to mould public opinion.
6—The Political party organizations of each nation, whether conservative, liberal, radical, socialist etc. existing in every country with parliamentary administration.
7—Internationally organized corruption, the white slave traffic, vice and drug-rings, etc.

Any one of the branches above enumerated has innumerable ramifications and the control of even the least of them cannot be obtained without money. Money therefore becomes one of the most powerful levers in the hands of men who form the controlling groups. Thus does research in the realm of Finance become indispensable to the students bent upon tracing the real power behind universal control. This power, they will find, is wholly in the hands of international Jewish financiers.

Glancing at the body frame of all political organizations, do we not perceive that MONEY is its main sinew? It would not sound preposterous to state that the electoral system is similar to that of auction, insomuch as it favours the highest bidder. In election campaigns, the successful candidate is not necessarily the most deserving or worthy of votes, but too frequently he who was able to buy the greater number of votes. Votes are captured by slogans, propaganda and, not unfrequently, bribery. Only an infinitesimal percentage among them will ever strive to find out the power or powers behind the candidate, and by whom he is, in effect, controlled.

Yet the importance of such an investigation is both obvious and necessary, for it is a proven fact that candidates to parliament in one country have sometimes been controlled by a man, or group of men, in another country inimical to their own.

If political control is international it must of necessity be subversive of PATRIOTISM. If it holds in its power the reckless forces of Socialism and Communism, it must be subversive of social order and the promoter of revolution.

If spiritual control is anti-christian, Gnostic and occult, it must be subversive of Christianity and Religion. If it directs vice rings of all kinds, it must aim at the destruction of the moral, intellectual and physical strength of the human Race.

If, in conclusion, Finance is Power and as such is concentrated in one point, it is the arbiter of War and Peace, Life and Death, Welfare and Wretchedness, Prosperity and Ruin.

Everything and, it is sad to say, almost everybody, has a price and can be bought though not always with money. Men who today wield financial power have, long since based their system of purchase on this axiom. Far be it from us to suggest that there are no idealists in every walk of life for whom the pursuit of either patriotism, religious mysticism or philanthropy is unadulterated. On the contrary, we shall go as far as to say that such people become the best tools in the hands of plotters by whom they are led to believe that disinterested material help will be given them for the attainment of their ideals or aims. The study of secret revolutionary societies will show many examples of remarkable cases of self-sacrifice on the part of genuine idealists. Subversives of either religious, social and political order have ever known how to make use of such people by instilling into them the super religion of the secret.

It is against this "secret" that the fight should be waged. If the aims of secret societies are good, one fails to see the need for their secret oaths and initiations. The "light" they promise should, like the sun, shine upon everyone.

To use the words of Christ: "Who lighteth a candle and putteth it under a bushel?"

Masonic and secret societies need light.

Hence, Light should be thrown upon them from without that their secrets may be revealed.

As to "Toleration"—indiscriminate toleration preached at random, it should be considered one of the exoteric bases upon which are erected subversive creeds.

Recognizing as they do the practical power of thought, sects induce their novices to surrender their use of this power whose normal function, guided by the individual conscience, is to discriminate between good and evil in order to oppose the latter. Thus they create a dangerous negative state of mind as opposed to the Christian or positive. The individual when robbed of his initiative can easily be swayed and guided by the will of others. Therein resides the power of hypnotism and in this wise the shibboleth of "toleration" which, in fact, paralyses opposition to evil, serves an esoteric purpose suspected by few.

If the contents of this book may help in safeguarding the young and the unwary against falling into the pitfalls set by agents of subversive sects, its author will not have laboured in vain.

The work is far from being completed. It claims, in fact, to be only an attempt in the direction of inexhaustible research work upon the coordination of the aims of all societies whether political or occult. It is to be hoped that others, and may they be many, will begin work where this book ends for—

"The harvest is great indeed but the labourers are few"

NOTES

1. The Autobiography of Wolfe Tone, p. 51.
2. The Autobiography of Wolfe Tone, p. 51.
3. Samuel Neilson (1761–1803), referred to in Tone's Autobiography as "The Jacobin". He was the founder of The Northern Star, the first organ of the society in the press.
4. The Autobiography of Wolfe Tone, op. cit., p. 242.
5. Ibid. p. 290.
6. Pollard, The Secret Societies of Ireland, p. 20.
7. Pollard, op. cit., p. 41.
8. Ibid. p. 125.
9. Ibid. p. 131.
10. Thomas Frost, The Secret Societies of the European Revolution, vol. I, p. 175.
11. The close connection between Grand Lodge and English Templarism, prior to 1791, is established in an article by T. B. Whytehead, in The Rosicrucian and Masonic Record, pp. 317 and 325.
12. Later Regent of France during the minority of Louis XV.
13. Heckethorn, Secret Societies of all Ages and Countries, vol. I, p. 302 et seq.
14. Stillson and Hughan, History of Freemasonry and Concordant Orders, p. 790.
15. Robert Freke Gould, The History of Freemasonry, vol. II, p. 135.
16. L. Fry, Waters Flowing Eastward.
17. L. Fry, Waters Flowing Eastward.

18. Gaston Cremieux, another member of the same family (1836–1871) was an active Socialist and Revolutionary. He participated in the Paris Commune and was court-martialed and executed in 1871.

19. "Union and Progress" was the name given to several revolutionary associations and also to several Masonic Lodges.

20. The means for the attainment of Crémieux's ambition are set forth in a book entitled Paris, Capitale des Religions, by Jean Izoulet.

21. P. B. Gheusi, Gambetta, Life and Letters, p. 207.

22. Pollard, The Secret Societies of Ireland, p. 32.

23. Pollard, op. cit., p. 35.

24. Ibid. p. 265.

25. Page 812 et seq.

26. Yarker traces Cerneau's patent to Henri Martin given by the Grand Lodge of France to supersede that of Morin in 1766. See The Arcane Schools, p. 482.

27. Stillson and Hughan, op. cit., p. 828.

28. Gargano, Irish and English Freemasons and their Foreign Brothers, p. 62, published 1878.

29. Carbonari conspiracy of Belforl and La Rochelle, p. 295.

30. Michael di Gargano, op. cit.

31. Revue Internationale des Societes Secretes, Sept. 2nd 1928, p. 809.

32. Ibid. p. 808.

33. Arrigo Solmi, The Making of Modern Italy, p. 25.

34. Heckethorn, Secret Societies of all Ages and Countries, vol. II, p. 145.

35. Ibid. pp. 110–111.

36. A history of the Hung is given in The Hung Society by J. S. Ward and W. G. Sterling.

37. A. E. Waite, Devil Worship in France, p. 254.

38. Secret Societies of Italy, London, p. 71.

39. Thomas Frost, The Secret Societies of the European Revolution, vol. II, p. 6.

40. Lucien de la Hodde, Histoire des Sociétés Secrètes

41. Heckethorn. Secret Societies of All Ages and Countries, vol. II, p. 175.

42. Also known as Levellers.

43. Pollard, Secret Societies of Ireland, p. 37.

44. "Inquire within", Light bearers of Darkness.

45. Harris married as one of his many wives the widow of the murdered Mason, William Morgan.

46. Blanchard, Scottish Rite Masonry, vol. I, p. 380.

47. Enc. Brit., Art. Mormons.

48. Enc. Brit., 9th Ed. Art. Mormonism.

49. Stuart Martin, The Mystery of Mormonism.

50. Blanchard 33°, op. cit., vol. II, p. 373.

51. Jewish Encyclopaedia, Art. B'nai B'rith.

52. Les Cahiers de l'Ordre, November 1927.

53. Pollard, The Secret Societies of Ireland, p. 10.

54. Pollard, op. cit., p. 44.

55. Pope Pius IX, on Nov. 15, 1848.

56. Pollard, op. cit., p. 46.

57. "Inquire Within", Light bearers of Darkness, p. 194 el seq.

58. The Complete Manual of Oddfellows, published 1879, p. 66.

59. Op. cit., p. 153.

60. John Drinkwater, Charles James Fox, p. 48.

61. Pollard, The Secret Societies of Ireland, p. 47.

62. Heckethorn, Secret Societies of All Ages and Countries, vol. II, p. 203.

63. Pollard, op. cit., p. 58 et seq.

64. Ibid. p. 60 et seq.

65. Pollard, op. cit, p. 67 et seq.

66. Revue Internationale des Societes Secrites, June 28, 1931.

67. Heckethorn, op. cit. vol. II, p. 224 et seq.

68. Heckethorn, op. cit.

69. Heckethorn, op. cit. p. 231.

70. Onslow Yorke, Secret History of the International, p. 66.

71. Heckethorn, op. cit., vol. II, p. 251 et seq.

72. Jewish Encyclopaedia, Article on Karl Marx.

73. Revue Internationale des Societes Secretes, June 28, 1931.

74. Dr. Wynn Westcott, M. W. Supreme Magus, History of The Societas Rosicruciana in Anglia, IX, privately printed, Dec. 30, 1900. Copyright. British Museum Press Mark 047 5 h54.

75. Part of these papers are presumed to be some of Nick Stone's rituals.

76. No. 1, July 1868, British Museum Press Mark 4782–h22.

77. "Inquire Within".

78. Latomia: One of the official periodicals of German Freemasonry.

79. Pollard, The Secret Societies of Ireland, p. 71 et seq.

80. United States of America.

81. Pollard, op. cit., p. 90 et seq.

82. Formed from The National Land League of America.

83. Pollard, op. cit., p. 98 et seq.

84. Pollard, op. cit., p. 134 el seq.

85. John Yarker, The Arcane Schools, p. 492.

86. Rene Guenon, Le Theosophisme, p. 293.

87. John Yarker, The Grand Mystic Temple.

88. Ibid.

89. Speculative Mason, July 1927, vol. 19.

90. Rene Guénon, Le Théosophisme, p. 12.

91. René Guénon, op. cit., p. 14.

92. "Inquire Within", Light-bearers of Darkness, p. 26.

93. René Guénon, op. cit., p. 21.

94. Inquire Within, op. cit., p. 26 et seq.

95. The Theosophist.

96. Papus (Docteur Encausse), Traite elementaire de Science Occulte, p. 147.
The following is a translation: "Each one of these adaptations being applicable
to the physical or spiritual world, one understands how real 'Illuminés' can draw
towards the light of truth, towards this 'light which lluminates all men coming
into this world', towards the divine living voice, the profanes called to initiation.
But for that it was necessary that the fundamental and hermetic key of the degrees
and their adaptation should be conserved by an occult university. Such was the role
that the Rose-Croix and the judeo-christians had reserved to themselves."

97. Sedir, Histoire des Rose-Croix, p. 124.

98. The International Bible Students Association, The Finished Mystery, p. 43,
    pub. 1918.

99. Pollard, The Secret Societies of Ireland, p. 82. For root of this movement see
    Chapter XCIV.

100. René Guénon, Le Theosophisme, p. 297.

101. John Yarker, The Arcane Schools, p. 429.

102. Hudson, The Law of Psychic Phenomena, p. 157.

103. See page 37 et seq.

104. Edward Maitland, Life of Anna Kingsford, Vol. II, p. 430. For root of this movement see Chapters LXXXVII, XCV.

105. Presented to the British Museum Library 5/11 /05, London. Privately printed Dec. 30th 1900, see p. 13.

106. Nesta Webster, Secret Societies, p. 311.

107. "Inquire Within", Light-bearers of Darkness, p. SG.

108. The German Organ of the Sect was The Oriflamme.

109. Article IV, Section 3, of the constitution of the O. T. O. provides that "The person (male or female) filling this office (head) shall serve for life or until his or her resignation" and Article IV, Section 4, provides that "The person filling this office shall appoint his or her successor."

110. The Master Therion, Magick, published 1930, p. 93.

111. Abbe Paul Boulain, Publisher, Les Étincelles, 26, rue de Bassano, Paris, 1929.

112. The Master Therion, op. cit., p. 97, Note.

113. The Master Therion, op. cit., p. 338.

114. Oupnek'hat, instruction 108, pages 85 and 92 of the first volume of the translation by Anquetil.

115. Richard Dawson, Red Terror and Green, p. 176.

116. Ibid. p. 185.

117. Officially connected with both Anti-saloon League and Council.

118. Officially connected with both Anti-saloon League and Council.

119. Officially connected with both Anti-saloon League and Council.

120. Officially connected with both Anti-saloon League and Council.

121. Officially connected with both Anti-saloon League and Council.

122. Officially connected with both Anti-saloon League and Council.

123. Officially connected with both Anti-saloon League and Council.

124. Officially connected with both Anti-saloon League and Council.

125. See Hearings before the Committee on the Judiciary, House of Representatives, and 71st Congress. The Prohibition Amendment, p. 546.

126. Since the foregoing was written, Tainted Contacts, by Col. Sanctuary, has been published and it fully bears out the truth of the above statements.

127. Sufism, Revue Philosophique Mensuelle, Feb. 1926.

128. George Kaufmann, Fruits of Anthroposophy, The Threefold Commonwealth, 74 Grosvenor St. W. London, 1922.

129. Captain Pollard, The Secret Societies of Ireland, p. 141.

130. The Ku-Klux Klan, Hearings before the Committee of Rules, House of Representatives, Sixty-seventh Congress, U. S. A. (1) p. 97.

131. Ibid. p. 102.

132. The Ku-Klux Klan, Hearings before the Committee of Rules, House of Representatives, Sixty-seventh Congress, U. S. A. (1) p. 91.

133. Ibid. p. 92.

134. Ibid. p. 122.

135. ibid. p. 123.

136. ibid. p. 75.

137. See the notes to the Small Maynard and Co. Boston edition of The Protocols published in 1920.

138. Nest a Webster, The Socialist Network, p. 44 et seq.

139. Recognition of Russia, p. 530, part 2.

140. The Prohibition Amendment. Hearings before the Committee Washington, 1930, 102788.

141. Data are from Anti-Saloon League Year book of 1929, published by the League, edited by Ernest H. Cherrington.

142. Officially connected with both League and Federal Council of Churches of Christ in America.

143. Officially connected with both League and Federal Council of Churches of Christ in America.

144. Officially connected with both League and Federal Council of Churches of Christ in America.

145. Officially connected with both League and Federal Council of Churches of Christ in America.

146. Officially connected with both League and Federal Council of Churches of Christ in America.

147. Officially connected with both League and Federal Council of Churches of Christ in America.

148. Officially connected with both League and Federal Council of Churches of Christ in America.

149. R. M. Whitney, The Reds in America, p. 120 et seq.

150. Op. cit., p. 56.

151. Jessie E. Sampter, Guide to Zionism, pp. 21, 87.

152. Leon Simon, op. rit., p. 120, Edition 1920.

153. Fred D. Pasley, Al Capone, p. 228.

154. L. Fry. Waters Flowing Eastward, Part II.

155. Torchbearers, p. C.

156. See pamphlet published by The American Defense Society Inc. 154 Nassau Street. New York City.

157. R. M. Whitney , The Youth Movement in America

158. See pamphlet issued by the Massachusetts Public Interest League, April, 1925.

159. Peace Militant, published by The New History Foundation New York City.